Royal Wedding

D0525867

Published by IPC Magazines Limited,
King's Reach Tower,
Stamford Street, London SE1 9LS
at the recommended price
shown on the frontispiece

Printed in England by Jarrold and Sons Limited
Whitefriars, Norwich NR3 1SH

ISBN 85037 382 4

£2.25

"It is with the greatest pleasure that The Queen and The Duke of Edinburgh announce the betrothal of their beloved son The Prince of Wales . . .

*. . . to the Lady Diana Spencer." These were the formal engagement pictures
taken at Buckingham Palace on February 24, 1981*

Written by Douglas Keay

Edited by Jane Reed and
Douglas Keay

Art Editors Keith Russell
Jack Clare

Production Editors Tony Skudder, Art
Peter Watson and
Jean Elgie, Editorial

Picture Editor Dennis Beaven

Picture Research Brian Mumford
Percy Hatchman

Publishers Jane Reed
James McMillan

Contents

His family tree

Master Peter
Phillips
(1977–   )

Prince Edward
(1964–   )

Prince Charles (1948–   )
m. Lady Diana Spencer (1961–   )

Prince Andrew
(1960–   )

Prince Michael
(1942–   )
m. Marie-Christine
von Reibnitz

Princess Anne (1950–   )
m. Capt. Mark Phillips

Elizabeth II (1926–   )
Reign 1952–
m. Prince Philip, Duke of
Edinburgh (1921–   )

Edward, Duke of Kent (1935–   )
m. Katharine Worsley

Princess Alexandra (1936–   )
m. Hon. Angus Ogilvy

Richard, Duke of Gloucester (1944–   )
m. Birgitte van Deurs

Alice (1885–1969)

Princess Margaret
(1930–   )
m. Antony
Armstrong-Jones
Earl of Snowdon

George,
Duke of Kent
(1902–1942)
m. Princess Marina
of Greece
(1906–1968)

Henry, Duke of Gloucester (1900–1974)
m. Lady Alice Montagu-Douglas-Scott

George VI (1895–1952)
Reigned 1936–1952
m. Lady Elizabeth Bowes-
Lyon (1900–   )

Edward VIII (1894–1972)
Reigned Jan.–Dec. 1936

George, Earl of
Harewood (1923–   )

Louis, Earl
Mountbatten
(1900–1979)
m. Hon. Edwina
Ashley

Mary, Princess Royal (1897–1965)
m. 6th Earl of Harewood (1882–1947)

Victoria Mary (1863–1950) m.
Louis of Battenberg 1st Marquess of
Milford Haven

George V (1865–1936)
Reigned 1910–1936
m. Princess Mary of Teck
(1867–1953)

Prince Arthur
(1850–1942)

Princess Alice (1843–1878)
m. Grand Duke of
Hesse (1837–1892)

Edward VII (1841–1910)
Reigned 1901–1910
m. Alexandra,
Princess of Denmark
(1844–1925)

Prince Alfred
(1844–1900)

Princess Helena
(1846–1923)

Prince Leopold
(1853–1884)

Princess Louise
(1848–1939)

Victoria (1819–1901)
Reigned 1837–1901
m. Prince Albert of Saxe-
Coburg-Gotha
(1819–1861)

Princess Victoria
(1840–1901)

Princess Beatrice
(1857–1944)

Her family tree

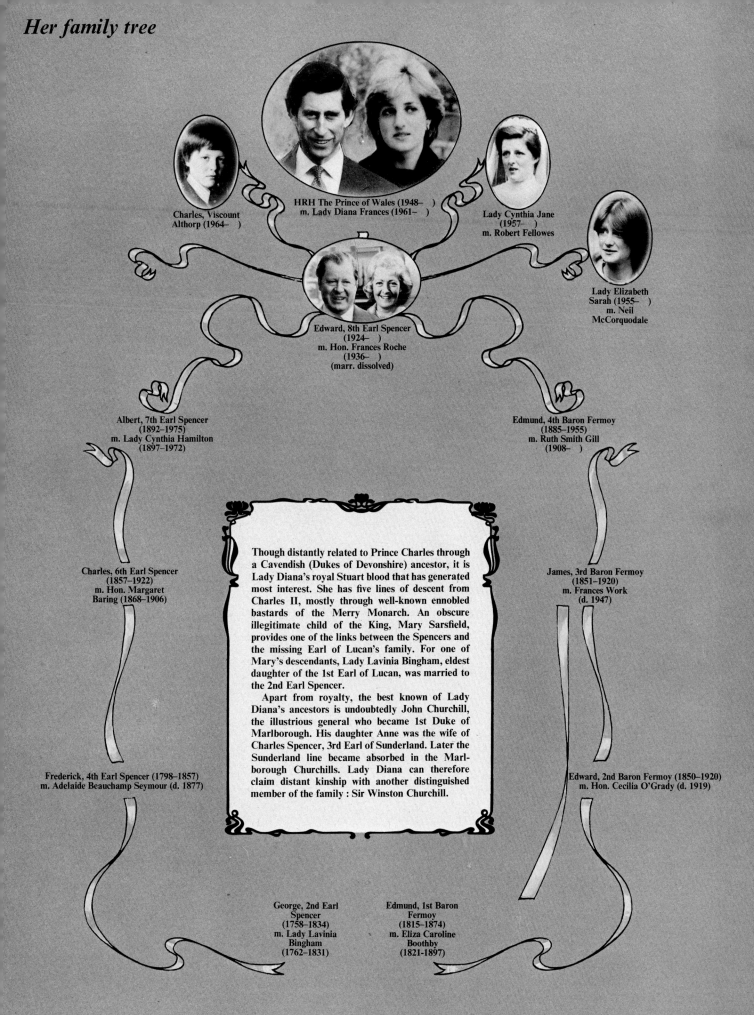

Charles, Viscount
Althorp (1964–   )

HRH The Prince of Wales (1948–   )
m. Lady Diana Frances (1961–   )

Lady Cynthia Jane
(1957–   )
m. Robert Fellowes

Lady Elizabeth
Sarah (1955–   )
m. Neil
McCorquodale

Edward, 8th Earl Spencer
(1924–   )
m. Hon. Frances Roche
(1936–   )
(marr. dissolved)

Albert, 7th Earl Spencer
(1892–1975)
m. Lady Cynthia Hamilton
(1897–1972)

Edmund, 4th Baron Fermoy
(1885–1955)
m. Ruth Smith Gill
(1908–   )

Charles, 6th Earl Spencer
(1857–1922)
m. Hon. Margaret
Baring (1868–1906)

James, 3rd Baron Fermoy
(1851–1920)
m. Frances Work
(d. 1947)

Though distantly related to Prince Charles through
a Cavendish (Dukes of Devonshire) ancestor, it is
Lady Diana's royal Stuart blood that has generated
most interest. She has five lines of descent from
Charles II, mostly through well-known ennobled
bastards of the Merry Monarch. An obscure
illegitimate child of the King, Mary Sarsfield,
provides one of the links between the Spencers and
the missing Earl of Lucan's family. For one of
Mary's descendants, Lady Lavinia Bingham, eldest
daughter of the 1st Earl of Lucan, was married to
the 2nd Earl Spencer.

Apart from royalty, the best known of Lady
Diana's ancestors is undoubtedly John Churchill,
the illustrious general who became 1st Duke of
Marlborough. His daughter Anne was the wife of
Charles Spencer, 3rd Earl of Sunderland. Later the
Sunderland line became absorbed in the Marlborough Churchills. Lady Diana can therefore
claim distant kinship with another distinguished
member of the family : Sir Winston Churchill.

Frederick, 4th Earl Spencer (1798–1857)
m. Adelaide Beauchamp Seymour (d. 1877)

Edward, 2nd Baron Fermoy (1850–1920)
m. Hon. Cecilia O'Grady (d. 1919)

George, 2nd Earl
Spencer
(1758–1834)
m. Lady Lavinia
Bingham
(1762–1831)

Edmund, 1st Baron
Fermoy
(1815–1874)
m. Eliza Caroline
Boothby
(1821–1897)

Diana's story

Once upon a time, the story should begin, there was a child born to rags who married a handsome, wealthy Prince.

But as everyone knows, Lady Diana Spencer was not born into a poor family, but to aristocrats who could trace their ancestry back as far as Charles II.

She was born on July 1, 1961—a child of the Sixties who was to grow into an Eighties girl, fair and free. A sprig of a family tree that had roots spreading deep into the history of England.

There were some black sheep, it is true—as in most families, ordinary as well as aristocratic. And some of the wealth in the coffers came from marriages into families with fortunes. In 1880, for instance, Frances Work, daughter of a New York millionaire, married the heir to the 2nd Baron Fermoy, Lady Diana's great-grandfather. On her father's side, there had been sheep farming, land and investment, and a superb art collection for a century and a half and more.

Back in the early 1700s there was the Hon. John Spencer—MP for Woodstock and Ranger of the Great Park of Windsor. He was the youngest son of the eminent statesman, the 3rd Earl of Sunderland, who in his turn was joint heir to John Churchill, the first and great Duke of Marlborough.

The Earls of Lucan were another branch of the family—there was Lord Lucan of the Charge of the Light Brigade fame and, more recently, the 7th Earl of Lucan who disappeared in 1974.

"God defend the right" is the somewhat ambiguous family motto of the Spencers, though there is no doubt it has all the stirring resonance to summon up visions of past chivalrous knights on horseback.

In this century, Spencers, Peels and Seymours—all inter-related—have stood service to the Royal Family in such honorary roles as Woman of the Bedchamber and Extra Lady-in-Waiting. Lady Diana's grandmother, Countess Spencer, who died in 1972, was Lady of the Bedchamber to the Queen Mother, and her other grandmother, Ruth, Lady Fermoy, is at present Woman of the Bedchamber and one of the Queen Mother's closest friends.

But all the ancestral rigmarole was of no concern, of course, to Diana when she arrived on the scene, the third daughter of Viscount and Viscountess Althorp. The Viscount was heir to the 7th Earl Spencer, and Diana's mother was the youngest daughter of Lord and Lady Fermoy.

Both the Althorps and the Fermoys were close friends of the whole Royal Family. The Althorps' home, Park House, where Diana spent her early childhood, was on the edge of the Sandringham estate. And the Althorps had a heated outdoor swimming pool, which the Royal Family didn't—not at Sandringham anyway. So, the story goes, on hot, summer days especially, the two families united in school holidays.

But few if any foresaw the day when little Diana might marry the Prince of Wales! For one thing, in the early Sixties, Charles was a shy, introverted boy of 14, about to be confronted with the rigours of Gordonstoun, while she was still a toddler, about to take her first faltering steps.

Lady Diana's sister, Elizabeth (known by

her second name, Sarah) was the eldest of the Althorp children, then came Cynthia (known as Jane). Diana Frances was the third, and Charles Edward Maurice, heir to the earldom, was born in May 1964, almost three years after Diana. Four children in nine years.

Unfortunately, the marriage was not destined to remain happy forever. As with most marriage breakdowns, probably no-one will ever know exactly why a couple who started out at 30 and 18 respectively with a wedding that was the social event of London society in 1954 should find, some 13 years later that it would be better all round if they did not remain together.

One day in 1967 the Althorp servants discovered that the mistress of the house "just was not there any more."

When the divorce was finalised in April 1969, Diana was only seven—old enough, as it is in most cases, to notice that what had mysteriously occurred made life different from what it had always been, yet young enough perhaps not to suffer the stabbing misery and insecurity that strikes some children in their teens.

There was acrimonious argument over who should have custody of the children—in the end this was awarded to Lord Althorp—

Far left: *At the age of seven, Lady Diana dons her Sunday best for the golden wedding celebrations of her grandfather, the 7th Earl Spencer*
Below: *The Spencers have always been close to the Royal Family. Here, at the wedding of the Duke of Kent to Katharine Worsley in 1961, Diana's elder sister, Lady Jane, is on the left and Princess Anne on the right*
Right: *Lady Diana, at 19, in London on the eve of her engagement*

and for a time their mother saw less of them than she would have wished.

Fortunate it was then, that during much of this time, Diana was a pupil at Riddlesworth Hall, a preparatory school housed in a rambling mansion, at Diss in Norfolk. There, amid the smells of polished floors and chalky blackboard dust, the atmosphere was warm, the teachers comforting if firm.

The headmistress at the time was Miss Elizabeth Ridsdale (nicknamed "Riddy" by the girls) who celebrated the silver jubilee of her headship during the three years that Diana was among her pupils.

Now retired, Miss Ridsdale has recalled a child who was active by nature, good at sports, especially swimming, and who loved horse riding. (Later Diana was to lose her riding nerve, as also happened to Prince Charles. But recently he has said he hopes to help her regain her confidence, in the way he has his own.)

Riddlesworth has always had an excellent reputation as a preparatory school for girls, with a high proportion of its pupils passing Common Entrance examinations to such prestigious schools as Benenden (Princess Anne's old school), Wycombe Abbey and Felixstowe.

However, it does not seem that Diana excelled particularly in academic subjects. What her old headmistress has recalled is "how sweet she was with the little ones."

In 1975, Lady Diana's father became the 8th Earl Spencer, when Diana was 14, and moved into the magnificent 16th-century ancestral home, Althorp House, in Northamptonshire.

Althorp has been the Spencers' family seat for 473 years. There is a 15,000 acre estate surrounding the huge mansion, which is open to the public at certain times of the year. And quite apart from any royal connections, the house is worth visiting for a sight of the paintings in the gallery and main rooms. Works by Gainsborough, Reynolds, Rubens, form part of one of the finest art collections in Britain, if not the world.

After prep school, Diana became a boarder at West Heath, near Sevenoaks, Kent—a school with an impeccable reputation for caring for its 130 pupils.

At Riddlesworth the children were encouraged to bring pet animals—a guinea pig or a rabbit—from home, house them in hutches provided at the school and feel consoled by them when they were homesick.

West Heath is for older girls, who are past such things, and the Australian headmistress, Miss Ruth Rudge, is regarded as being fair but firm, and holding to a traditional form of discipline.

Once again, it is not reported that Diana came out top of the school—but she was no dunce either!

Close members of the family have been reported as saying her school reports showed her to be "normal and average". And others remember her cheerful personality and willingness to help out. She was not a born leader, but never negative either.

Because of her parents' divorce and subsequent remarriages, her holidays were

Below: *Althorp, the family seat of the Spencers for 473 years. Surrounded by a 15,000 acre estate, the house contains a valuable collection of paintings by Gainsborough and Reynolds*
Right: *West Heath School, Sevenoaks, Kent, at which Lady Diana was a boarder before leaving at 16 for a finishing school in Switzerland*

divided. Her mother had married Peter Shand Kydd, whose family were in the wallpaper business. They now live on a farm on the island of Seil on the west coast of Scotland. In 1976, her father married Raine, the former Countess of Dartmouth and daughter of romantic novelist Barbara Cartland.

Diana has always been fond of both her parents, but as the years passed it was her mother who became the more central character in her life.

At West Heath school—where Queen Mary, wife and consort of George V, was once a pupil—Lady Diana shared a dormitory with five other girls. On the wall between the windows, almost by chance, was a colour photograph of Prince Charles,

taken at his investiture as Prince of Wales in 1969, and presented to the school by former newspaper chief, Cecil King.

West Heath school, founded 116 years ago and where fees run to nearly £2,800 a year, is set among 32 acres of Kent countryside. It aims to provide a sound general education and to allow its pupils to "develop their own minds and tastes and to realise their duties as citizens."

By all accounts, Lady Diana enjoyed her lessons, even though they didn't finish until seven in the evening, with an extra session on Saturday morning. *And* she had to be up by 7.30 a.m. each day.

Staff and former pupils at West Heath will always hold memories of a girl with longish hair and a fringe who did not outshine

anyone else in exam results, but who was always cheerful and helpful—the kind of girl who, if she saw something that needed doing, such as tidying up a room, would get on with it without being asked, while her more studiously minded classmates talked on endlessly.

Unlike most of her companions, Lady Diana did not stay on to take university entrance exams. After just three years at West Heath school, at 16, she was "off" again—as her Sloane Square friends would put it. This time to Switzerland and the exclusive Institut Alpin Videmanette in Rougemont—a finishing school for the children of wealthy European families, where the aim is to make the young ladies "healthy and happy by ensuring they work

hard and play hard in a relaxed family atmosphere."

There was very little free time to escape to the nearby jet-set resort of Gstaad, and even when there were school outings, the girls were always chaperoned.

These restrictions, quite normal in such establishments, must even so have irked some of the pupils who, back home, would probably have been "disco-ing" the nights away. Lady Diana herself may have wished she was older and school days over—almost certainly on the occasion when, across the mountains at Klosters, Prince Charles took her eldest sister, Lady Sarah, with him on a ski-ing holiday.

Though they must have known of each other's existence since childhood, it was

Lady Sarah who formally re-introduced Prince Charles to her youngest sister, when she was 16 and he was almost 29, at a weekend shoot on her father's estate. Later Prince Charles was to recall thinking what "a splendid 16-year-old" she was, "and full of fun".

However, there were no thoughts of romance then. If anything, as Lady Diana inferred on her engagement day, the expectation was stronger that she and Prince Andrew might automatically see more of each other, because they are nearer in age— "I always ganged up with Prince Andrew," she said.

By early 1978, school days were nearly over for Lady Diana. She had been expected to return to the Institut in Switzerland after

the Easter holidays for the summer term. But, with the snow gone, so was Lady Diana.

The question that then arose was—what is Diana to do now?

Parents of wealthy and/or aristocratic families in Britain are not renowned for being particularly concerned about whether or not their teenage daughters work towards and plan professional careers. There are exceptions, of course. The Duke and Duchess of Wellington's daughter, Lady Jane Wellesley, herself once tipped to marry the Prince of Wales, is a case in point—she has built up an excellent reputation in television as a researcher and potential producer.

Up until 30 years ago, however, the vast majority of "gals from good homes", as they were condescendingly termed by the less blue-blooded, were expected to "come out" in a London season of cocktail parties and grand balls. The ultimate goal, they were left in no doubt, was marriage to a "suitable" person. And once the objective was achieved they and their spouses retired once more to the country, generally to a house surrounded by vast acres, there to bring up three or four children, and cope as best they could with the decimation of family fortune brought about by death duties.

Such a future might still have been the lot of Lady Diana and her contemporaries, had it not been for the effects of the social upheaval of the 1960s, the effects of which penetrated even to the most conservative corners of the shires, like an irritating and inescapable draught, or a breath of fresh air, depending on where one was placed.

By the mid-Seventies, girls with family backgrounds such as Diana's were working in posh boutiques. They made up mini-bus parties to India, cooked and served in-office lunches for City executives, worked as secretaries or au-pairs, and flat-shared with other girls, and sometimes young men. The word unisex became as commonly used as "U" and "non-U" had been 20 years earlier.

In Lady Diana's case, the future after she returned from Switzerland was complicated by the fact that her father had re-married (none of his daughters was present at the wedding) and had been struck down by a massive brain haemorrhage. Raine, his wife, moved heaven and earth to get him the best treatment, including securing a drug from Germany which she believes saved her husband's life.

But Earl Spencer required quiet and constant attention for many months still. There was very little that his youngest daughter could do in addition to help those surrounding her father, and so it was thought as well that she should be living in London, sharing a flat bought by Earl Spencer, with three of her girlfriends, Virginia Pitman, 21, a cordon bleu cookery student, Carolyn Pride, 19, a music student, and Anne Bolton, 21.

For a time Lady Diana thought of taking an advanced cookery course—she is not at all bad, it's said, at preparing an excellent meal. And for a while she looked after the handicapped child of an American couple.

But the job she was best known for doing

up until this point was that of nursery assistant at the Young England School in Pimlico, a once poor, but nowadays fashionable area of London, not a couple of miles from Buckingham Palace.

Everyone who knows her speaks of Lady Diana's love for children—working at the kindergarten was the one part of her life that she admitted she would miss after the announcement of her engagement. Chums at her old school in Kent say she often expressed a desire to have a large family of her own one day.

Her temperament seems ideally suited to coping with the tantrums of small children. She can be firm when necessary, giving a sharp glance from the corner of her eye. But almost any reproach is quickly followed by a smile and, very often, a giggle. She's not the sort of person who, without meaning to, goes into a paddy when a child misbehaves and, worse, goes *on* misbehaving. Children tend to be quickly at ease in her company, and she, for her part, appears to be just as relaxed in their company; interested in what they're doing, ready to help, when help is needed, intrigued to compare one child's development with that of another. To her, one feels, children would never be merely appendages, brought down from the nursery by nanny to say a respectful goodnight to their parents.

When her day's work at the kindergarten was over, the mugs washed up, the toys stacked away, and the children picked up at the gate by mothers or nannies, "Miss Diana", as she was known to the children, would either drive back to her flat in South Kensington in her small car (the one she had before she acquired her famous Mini-Metro), or, especially when the weather was fine, ride back on her bicycle through dusty London streets.

In the evenings there would be tights to rinse through, things to iron, snack meals to cook, phone calls to make and answer, chats—some hurried, some long and leisurely—with the other girls in the flat, television programmes not to be missed, and television programmes to slump in front of. And laughter, lots of laughter.

There would be evenings out at the theatre, or at the ABC cinema down the road. Dates for meals in wine bars. Drinks with friends in pubs—"gin with lots and lots of tonic, please"—and going away parties and coming home celebrations at the flats of young people who seemed to be always "popping off" to or "floating in from" Australia, America, or wherever.

And whenever the opportunity arose, dancing. Lady Diana loves dancing.

At the weekends there was stocking-up at the local supermarket, and present-buying at Harrods. Fortnum and Mason for coffee or tea perhaps, and a wander through fabric-laden Liberty's. Phone calls and letters to her mother in Scotland, occasionally arranging to meet up in London.

There was also driving up motorways, or taking the train. Invitations to Balmoral, going to visit friends in the country, and going home to see father.

One place you'd rarely find Lady Diana

Far left: *The picture that winged its way round the world to almost every newspaper. When rumours first abounded of a new romance in Prince Charles' life, Lady Diana agreed to pose for a photographer who called at the Young England School in Pimlico, London, where she taught the kindergarten children. Shot against the light, when the picture appeared it showed the sun streaming through her cotton skirt—and caused her much amused embarrassment*
Top left: *Police keep an eye on Lady Diana's*

flat in the Old Brompton Road, South Kensington, where she lived with three girlfriends up until her engagement, when she moved to Clarence House
Top right: *Lady Diana's natural and caring love of children was quickly recognised at the kindergarten where she worked*
Above *Two of the three young women who shared Lady Diana's London flat: Carolyn Pride, 19 and Virginia Pitman, 21. Earl Spencer bought the flat, so that Diana could have a base in London*

Spencer, aged 18, was in smart London night clubs, or in clever-dick gossip columns.

And then everything changed . . .

In July 1980, she was a guest at Balmoral during the Royal Family's summer holidays. Not such an unusual occurrence for a friend of the family, and in any case, the main purpose of the visit was to help her sister Lady Jane (wife of Robert Fellowes, the Queen's Assistant Private Secretary), with her first baby. But later, Prince Charles and Lady Diana were both to admit that this was the period when their romance had begun.

"We began to realise then that there was something in it," said Prince Charles.

For once, Fleet Street was a little slow on the up-take, but on September 8 one newspaper proclaimed "IN LOVE AGAIN: Lady Diana is the new girl for Charles."

She was described, somewhat unflatteringly, as a shoulder to cry on following the well-publicised split between Prince Charles and the strong-willed Anna Wallace.

With a new girl on the scene, the reporters started digging once more, and when they discovered Lady Diana taught at a kindergarten, the school was besieged by photographers. There is something very appealing to newspaper editors and their readers about a Prince's girlfriend who is doing a useful job, and one who works with photogenic children, what's more.

Instead of running away, or losing her temper, Lady Diana displayed kindness and good sense at the sudden interest in her, and even agreed to pose for a few minutes for a photographer—in the hope, forlornly, that that would be that.

She was devastated when she saw among the published pictures one that was shot against the light, showing the sun streaming through her cotton skirt.

But this was only the beginning. In the coming months she was to be besieged, bothered, but miraculously never seemingly bewildered, by the newsmen and women who lay in wait for her at almost every turn.

Prince Charles worried, as always with any of his friends, about Lady Diana having to contend with Press interest—"I have people to protect me from that sort of thing." But there was not much he could do, short of announcing an engagement, and the romance hadn't reached that stage yet.

What impressed everyone, not least those at Buckingham Palace, was the accomplished manner in which Lady Diana answered reporters' questions. She didn't give away the slightest hint of a romance (except by her obvious happiness perhaps), but there was nothing superior or nervous about her manner. Millions watching the television news saw her, surrounded by media, calmly go to her car, exchange a few words with a reporter, smile, giggle, and get in. And in just those few seconds millions were saying to themselves, "She seems a very sweet girl. Nice sense of humour. I wonder if Prince Charles *will* marry her."

Those months of speculation, however well handled, cannot have been easy for Lady Diana. She is not a natural show-off. But like the Queen Mother as a young

Far left: *This picture was taken in November 1980, when Press speculation about a possible marriage between Prince Charles and Lady Diana was growing by the day. Somehow, at 19, Lady Diana managed to keep her composure, even in the face of television news reporters and cameras* **(above)**. *At this stage, Buckingham Palace could hardly afford to think in terms of protection against legitimate Press interest without increasing speculation. In contrast, Prince Charles, on an official tour of India* **(right)**, *was surrounded by ceremony*

woman, to whom she has often been compared, she apparently has a strong will, self-containment, and an instinctive flair for the best way to react to the unexpected.

She also displayed, at times, a nifty ability to throw the Press off the scent, by switching cars or not turning up where she was expected to turn up.

Without any official protection or guidance from Buckingham Palace, Lady Diana tried her best to carry on her private life with humour and tolerance.

But the stage was reached when her mother thought enough was enough. "May I ask the editors of Fleet Street," she wrote to The Times, "whether, in the execution of their jobs, they consider it necessary or fair to harass my daughter daily, from dawn until well after dusk?"

For a few days after that, the pursuit did slacken pace. Prince Charles was on a tour of India, and when he returned just before Christmas, Lady Diana was unluckily on the verge of going down with flu.

In January, however, when the Royal Family went to Sandringham, newsmen once again were as thick on the ground as pheasants, and almost as well hidden.

Prince Charles greeted one covey with "A very happy New Year—and to your editors a particularly nasty one." It was an uncharacteristically harsh remark for him to make, and it gave pause to the speculators.

Had they got it all wrong—again?

No, was the answer. Their always fragile confidence was restored only four days later when Prince Charles and Lady Diana were reported as having met for a dawn rendezvous at a Berkshire stables—before Prince Charles dashed off to the funeral of the 97-year-old Princess Alice, Countess of Athlone. A stable lad told reporters: "They seemed very happy together. Like a couple in love, laughing and joking."

The day before, they had "camped out" together for lunch at Prince Charles' new and scarcely furnished country house in Gloucestershire, and the following weekend the Palace confirmed that Lady Diana had joined the Royal Family for a three-day stay at Sandringham. It seemed almost safe enough now for newspapers to go ahead with plans, begun long ago (with the bride's name left blank), to print souvenir editions celebrating the engagement. But *certain* knowledge was what was wanted, and as we now know, it was one of Prince Charles' greatest private ambitions to prevent anyone "scooping" the news of his engagement.

One evening, at the beginning of February, Lady Diana and Prince Charles shared a light dinner in the sitting-room of his private apartments at Buckingham Palace. And it was during that evening that the heir to the Throne proposed. He did not necessarily expect a firm answer, for he was aware that Lady Diana planned a short holiday with her mother in Australia and "I wanted to give her a chance to think about it—to think if it was all going to be too awful." But, as Lady

Diana told the same court correspondent, "I never had any doubts about it."

But she did go to Australia all the same. And the Press once more attempted to track her down. This time they failed. The security was tight. Even Prince Charles, when he phoned Lady Diana, had difficulty in persuading those who filtered the calls that he was in fact the Prince of Wales. "They all give us that story," said the voice at the other end, assuming Prince Charles was a reporter!

Another phone call made by Prince Charles was to Lord Spencer, formally asking for the hand of his daughter in marriage ("I don't know what would have happened if I'd said 'No'").

Prince Charles also informed the Queen and Prince Philip of his plans.

When Lady Diana returned from Australia, refreshed but even more certain of her love, she was given preferential treatment coming through Heathrow Airport.

On the Sunday, Prince Charles and Lady Diana entertained her father and stepmother over drinks at Buckingham Palace.

On the Monday evening she visited the Palace once more.

And on Tuesday, February 24, at 11 a.m., a statement from the Palace announced that "It is with the greatest pleasure that The Queen and The Duke of Edinburgh announce the betrothal of their beloved son The Prince of Wales . . ."

The story of Lady Diana Spencer was only just beginning . . .

A new life

At a conservative estimate, some 700 million people around the world will watch television coverage of the Royal wedding in St. Paul's Cathedral on July 29. And they will see it repeated again and again until every detail has been imprinted on their minds.

When Lady Diana woke up on February 24, 1981, it was not only to the morning of her official engagement, it was also to the start of a completely new life. A life in which she would be protected, surrounded and, at times, almost suffocated by protocol.

The first reaction of many people was joy that Prince Charles had at last found such a beautiful bride, and the first question that sprang to several minds was: "Can a young woman of only 19 possibly realise what a responsibility she's taking on?"

Lady Diana gave the answer within the day, "Next to Prince Charles, I can't go wrong. He's there with me."

Prince Charles was quite sure "she will be very, very good." He pointed out that he was about the same age, or only a little older, when he first began the almost continuous round of public duties. "It's obviously difficult to start with, but you just have to plunge in." (He was momentarily forgetting, perhaps, that he had been born to the job.)

In the space of a night and a day Lady Diana was whisked from a shared flat in South Kensington to a suite of rooms in Clarence House. And instead of using her Mini-Metro, she found herself being chauffeur-driven with an armed police officer at her side.

But these were the sort of changes she had expected. Just as she was aware that now it would be virtually impossible to go anywhere without being recognised.

Like any bride, there have been a million things to do, and she wasn't sure where to begin. Or where to stop. She has had to remind herself that she now has an efficient organisation behind her.

Prince Charles was due to leave for New Zealand, Australia, Venezuela and America barely a month after their engagement—but again, she was conscious that painful separations would be a part of her new life.

Of the many decisions that are being made about the life of the future Princess of Wales, surely one of the wisest was to accept the Queen Mother's invitation for Lady Diana to stay with her until the wedding day.

There could be no-one better suited to be close at this time to the girl who is to marry her favourite grandson. And when the great day arrives she will know just how Diana feels, having experienced it all herself. For she, too, came from comparative obscurity to fall in love with a prince of the Royal blood, and marry a future king.

Above left: *The Earl and Countess Spencer outside Buckingham Palace on the day of the engagement*
Inset: *Mrs. Shand Kydd, Lady Diana's mother*
Left: *Chief Inspector Paul Officer, at the wheel, taking care of Lady Diana*
Right: *Engagement night, and dinner at Clarence House*

His parents' marriage

Above: *After the wedding, waving from the balcony of Buckingham Palace*

Left: *The formal wedding picture of a supremely happy Princess Elizabeth and Prince Philip, a lieutenant in the Royal Navy*
Below: *On the way to Westminster Abbey, Princess Elizabeth and her father, King George VI, pass through Trafalgar Square*

Prince Charles' parents fell in love when the Queen, then Princess Elizabeth, was around 18 and her husband-to-be was a naval lieutenant serving in World War II.

For some time King George VI and Queen Elizabeth thought their daughter was too young to marry, and took her on a three-month royal tour of South Africa. But about two months after their return the engagement was announced and the date of the wedding was set: November 20, 1947.

Most people welcomed the celebrations and spectacle of a royal wedding as a relief from the boring austerity of post-war Britain with its petrol rationing, food shortages and not even television to rush home to.

The wedding itself took place in Westminster Abbey on a typically cold and wet November day. There were eight bridesmaids, including Princess Margaret and Princess Alexandra, and two pages, the little Princes, William of Gloucester and Michael of Kent.

The bride's gown was designed, in great secrecy, by Norman Hartnell, and inspired by "a Botticelli figure in clinging ivory silk, trailed with jasmine, smilax, syringa and small white rose-like blossoms."

Prince Philip made a dashing figure in naval uniform, with five rows of decorations, and a ceremonial sword. Only recently given British nationality—he was born the only son of Prince Andrew of Greece—he had the Marquess of Milford Haven, a fellow Naval officer, as best man. King George VI, a pale, slender man less than five years from the end of his life, brought his elder daughter to the altar while the congregation in Westminster Abbey rose to the sound of one of the bride's favourite hymns: Praise My Soul, The King of Heaven.

"Notwithstanding the splendour and national significance of the service in this Abbey," said the Archbishop of Canterbury in his address, "it is in all essentials the same as it would be for any cottager who might be married this afternoon in some small country church in a remote village in the dales. The same vows are taken, the same prayers are offered, and the same blessings are given."

It was true, and yet it was not. Few weddings could have been as richly splendid as this one. But there were moments which were unrehearsed and not included in any plan. As when, just before the wedding march, Princess Elizabeth, now wife but still a daughter, sank billowing in a deep and grateful curtsy to her father, the King.

At Buckingham Palace 150 guests sat down to the wedding breakfast, with its four-tier cake weighing 500 lb. Beside each plate was a sprig of white heather from Balmoral.

When the bride and groom left for their honeymoon, the weather had turned so cold that the open carriage that took them to Waterloo station was padded in with hot water bottles.

The first night was spent at Broadlands, the Hampshire home of the bridegroom's uncle, Lord Louis Mountbatten. But for the main part of the honeymoon Princess Elizabeth and her husband travelled to Birkhall, the King's house on Deeside, where Elizabeth had enjoyed many summer holidays and where, in future years, Prince Charles was often to visit his grandmother, Queen Elizabeth the Queen Mother.

Above: *The royal wedding cake, made by McVitie and Price and weighing all of 500 lb.*

Below: *The bride and bridegroom, the best man, the bridesmaids and the Royal Family. On Prince Philip's left is Princess Margaret, and on the left of the front row is the bride's grandmother, Queen Mary, who was not to live long enough to see the coronation of her granddaughter in 1953*

Her parents' marriages

It was the highlight of the social calendar of 1954—the wedding at Westminster Abbey of Viscount Althorp, heir to Earl Spencer, and the Hon. Frances Roche, beautiful debutante daughter of Lord and Lady Fermoy. He was 30 and she was 18—practically the same age difference exists between Prince Charles and Lady Diana.

The Queen, the Queen Mother, Princess Margaret and Princess Alexandra were among the guests, numbering over 1,500, who arrived at the West Door of the Abbey at 2 p.m. on a chilly, drizzly June day.

The bride set out from her parents' home in fashionable Belgravia. Her bridal gown was of white faille, embroidered on the tight-fitting bodice and full skirt with hand-cut diamanté, sequins and rhinestones. A white tulle veil, held in place by a simple diamond tiara belonging to her mother, formed a short train.

The three pages wore white satin suits with pale blue sashes, modelled after a painting by Reynolds, and the bridesmaids and attendants (Wake-Walker, Cholmondeley, Astor, Roche, Fogg-Elliot, Douglas-Home and Combe), wore white spotted muslin dresses with fichu necklines and blue moiré sashes.

At the time, the bridegroom was acting Master of the Royal Household and just after his engagement to Frances Roche was announced, he was required to accompany the Queen on an overseas tour lasting six months. But on the way home the Queen gave him leave to fly ahead, to help with the arrangements for the wedding.

Sadly, 13 years later, the marriage was over. Lord and Lady Althorp were living apart, he at his home in Sandringham, she in a flat in Chelsea. Their four children—Sarah, Jane, Diana and Charles—were then aged 12, 10, 6 and 3.

In April 1968, the London Evening News reported that Mrs. Janet Elizabeth Shand Kydd had been granted a divorce on the ground of adultery by her husband, Peter, with Lady Althorp, aged 32. Following the Althorps' divorce in 1969, Lady Diana's mother married Peter Shand Kydd.

And in July 1976 Earl Spencer, formerly Lord Althorp, married the former Lady Dartmouth, aged 46, daughter of romantic novelist Barbara Cartland. At the time Lady Diana Spencer was 15 years old.

Left: *The wedding at Westminster Abbey of Viscount Althorp to the Honourable Frances Burke Roche was the society event of 1954. The guard of honour was formed by NCOs of the bridegroom's regiment, the Royal Scots Greys*
Right: *After a reception at St. James's Palace attended by some 700 guests, the bride and bridegroom set off for their honeymoon in Italy and Austria*
Top right: *The 18-year-old bride carried a bouquet of lilies of the valley, white roses and stephanotis*
Above: *Earl Spencer, formerly Viscount Althorp, with his second wife, Raine, daughter of the famous romantic novelist Barbara Cartland*

Birth and babyhood

The news that Princess Elizabeth and the Duke of Edinburgh were expecting their first baby came on the eve of Derby Day, 1948. In the manner of the times, the official announcement was almost coyly oblique: "Her Royal Highness, The Princess Elizabeth, Duchess of Edinburgh, will undertake no public engagements after the end of June." The next day, at the Epsom races, crowds surged round Princess Elizabeth's car, cheering and shouting their congratulations.

King George VI's first grandchild would be the first child to be born in direct succession to the Throne in 54 years, and the story goes that Princess Elizabeth deliberately relined the family crib in buttercup yellow silk, so no-one would guess whether she and her husband wanted a boy or a girl.

Prince Charles was born during the evening of November 14, 1948, in a room at Buckingham Palace that had been used only a few days previously for an examination on the arteries in the King's leg.

Because of King George VI's insistence there was not a government minister present in the room at the time of the birth—as, by centuries-old tradition, there had been at previous royal confinements. The baby's father was not there either. Prince Philip was taking his mind off things by playing squash in the Palace squash court.

When the good news was brought to him he bounded up the stairs, first to the sitting-room where the King and Queen were waiting, then to the room where the Princess was still drowsy from the anaesthetic, then to the nursery where his son—who weighed 7 lb. 6 oz. at birth—was sleeping. When Princess Elizabeth did regain consciousness her first sight was of her husband, standing proudly at her bedside, with a huge bouquet of roses and carnations.

The Prince was christened on December 15, and because the Palace chapel still lay wrecked as a result of a German dive-bomber attack eight years earlier, a font—made for the baptism of Queen Victoria's first child in 1840—was brought from Windsor and set up in the music room.

The announcement that the Prince was to be named Charles did cause some surprise. It had not been borne by a reigning monarch since Charles II, who died in 1685, and some

supposed that Princess Elizabeth consciously wished to revive the royal Stuart names. It was not so. It was simply that she and her husband liked the name Charles, just as they liked the name Anne—the Stuart name they were to give their second child.

Prince Charles spent the first few months of his life in Buckingham Palace, principally because the house being prepared for his parents—Clarence House—had taken so long to get ready. Once the home of the Duke of Clarence, who became William IV (and now the London home of the Queen Mother), Clarence House looks across the Mall to St. James's Park and is only a short walk away from Buckingham Palace itself.

Two maids kept the nursery tidy, a nursery footman brought food up from the kitchen, and two nannies—Helen Lightbody and Mabel Anderson—looked after the Prince and wheeled his pram in Green Park. Prince

Far left: *The Queen with her one-month-old son, Prince Charles Philip Arthur George. The picture was taken at Buckingham Palace by Sir Cecil Beaton*
Left: *A stalwart young man with, for some unaccountable reason, a broom over his shoulder*
Above: *This picture was taken at Balmoral, the holiday home Prince Charles has grown to love so much*
Right: *The first photograph of Charles with his parents, when he was 19 weeks old*
Below: *An early conversation piece between Prince Charles and his sister Anne*

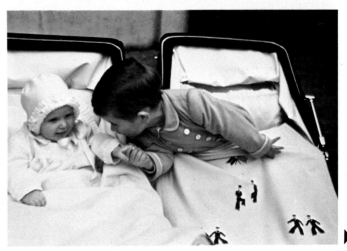

BIRTH AND BABYHOOD *continued*

Charles' first memory is of sitting up in that pram and thinking to himself what a great distance there was between him and the hands pushing him along.

Another memory he retains is of his great-grandmother, Queen Mary, who—although she had never allowed anyone else—used to let him play with some of the precious objects, collected over a lifetime, that were kept in glass-fronted cabinets. Prince Charles was only four when Queen Mary died, a courageous lady who lived to see her husband and three of her sons die, and another abdicate the Throne.

Charles was less than two years old when his sister Princess Anne arrived. Their father was a serving Royal Naval officer, then commanding the frigate Magpie, and their mother, because of the worsening illness of George VI, was increasingly busy with royal engagements.

Even so, nothing was allowed to get in the way of the children being taken to her at nine o'clock each morning. And in the evening she always set aside an hour-and-a-half to play with them, bath them, and tuck them up in bed.

When Prince Charles was only three years old, his mother became Queen. And though he has no memory of her coronation, in June, 1953, he is supposed to have said, at the end of the momentous day: "There won't be another coronation for a long time, and that will be mine."

Above: *Ahead of his time, Prince Charles takes the salute from Buckingham Palace after the Trooping the Colour, 1953*
Left: *Blowing the huntsman's horn, in 1955*
Below: *In May 1954, Prince Charles and Princess Anne were presented to the famous Barbary Apes on the Rock of Gibraltar*
Bottom: *A series of pictures for the family album, taken at Windlesham Moor in 1949*

24

Above: *On board Britannia, on her maiden voyage. Prince Charles was sailing out to Tobruk to be reunited with the Queen and Prince Philip, after their world tour following the Queen's coronation*
Right: *The familiar wave that was to be repeated a million times in the coming years*
Below: *Using one of his mother's cameras, the boy Prince tries his hand at photography*

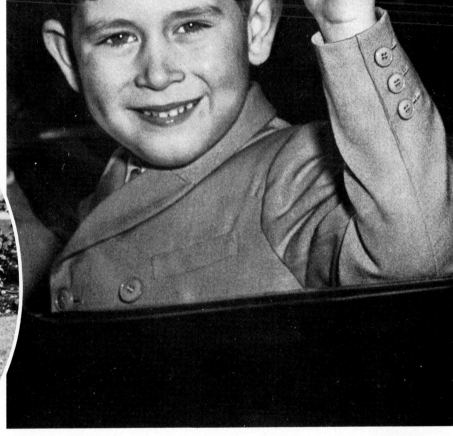

The grandfather he hardly knew

The picture on the left holds a special place in the affection of the Queen, and for many years now it has stood framed on her desk at Balmoral Castle.

Taken on Charles' third birthday, it shows a typically lively little boy sitting on a sofa next to a very proud grandfather. It is the only real memory that Prince Charles retains of King George VI who, at the time, was already a sick man with less than three months to live.

Mingled with the memory is an impression of another man—besides the photographer—swinging a shiny watch attached to a chain. This was in fact Sir Richard Colville, the Palace Press Secretary, who was trying to keep the boy still for long enough to have the photograph taken.

The Queen, then Princess Elizabeth, was on a tour across Canada with Prince Philip when the picture was taken and it was a pleasing surprise on their return.

Prince Charles was thought much too young to attend his grandfather's funeral in February 1952. Both he and Princess Anne remained at Sandringham to avoid the possibility of their glimpsing the mournful and majestic funeral procession as it moved along the Mall and then passed Clarence House where Princess Elizabeth and her family then lived.

Observers have sometimes remarked on the resemblance between Prince Charles and King George VI when he was a young man—especially when Prince Charles was serving with the Royal Navy and wearing a beard, like his grandfather had done at a similar period in his life. But it is in character that they most resemble one another—though fortunately Charles has not inherited his grandfather's temper, which could be fearsome at times. More important, through his mother and her father he has inherited those qualities of both friendliness and unswerving dedication which have earned both monarchs love and respect from succeeding generations of subjects.

Left: *The famous picture of King George VI and his first grandson,*
that for many years has stood
on the Queen's desk
at Balmoral
Oval: *Four generations of the Royal Family in one picture, taken at*
the christening of Prince Charles in December 1948.
On the right is Queen Mary,
widow of George V, and standing behind,
her second son, King George VI
Above right: *Prince Charles holds his grandmother's hand, while the nanny holds Princess Anne. The family had just arrived at Ballater,*
the nearest railway station to Balmoral
Right: *During the same 1951 holiday at Balmoral Castle, Prince Charles sits astride the sculpture of a deer while his grandfather*
holds on to Princess Anne's pram.
On the right, next to the Queen Mother,
is Princess Margaret

Right: *The Queen Mother with her first grandchild, following his christening at Buckingham Palace. The infant Prince is wearing the same robe of Honiton lace used by successive generations of the Royal Family since 1842, and the christening of Queen Victoria's second child* **Above:** *Waving to the crowds from a window of Clarence House on the Queen Mother's 55th birthday*

A proud grandmother

Prince Charles is the kind of young man who is very good with old people. He genuinely likes them, and venerates age in a way that many other young people would think sentimental and even out of date.

And although this is not the reason he is so fond of his maternal grandmother, it is certainly a contributory factor.

Denied a grandfather with the death of King George VI when Prince Charles was only three, he found in the Queen Mother an exceptionally devoted grandmother. Because his mother came to the Throne when she was still young, and had to spend much of her time away from home, Charles saw more of his grandmother than he might otherwise have done, and the strong bond which formed early on has never weakened.

The Queen Mother is not an interfering person. She leads very much an independent life. But at the same time she has always kept a close eye on her family, watching their characters develop, spotting weaknesses as well as strengths and tracing their origins to generations past. She seldom criticises, but when she does the slightest, generally good-natured, rebuke invariably goes home. She praises sparingly, knowing how much her commendation counts and how easily a young head can be swollen. She is always there, like all good grannies, to be turned to when needed. And she is never, or rarely, on the scene when she thinks things will go better without the presence of an old lady.

Her pride in her eldest grandson has, if anything, increased with the years. She has seen him grow up into not only a fine and popular Prince but into someone who in several ways resembles her late husband. Like King George VI, Charles has had to overcome shyness. He is extremely thoughtful and caring of how people feel. He is essentially a gentle person. All these qualities the Queen Mother loved in her husband, and now sees reflected in her grandson.

In addition there are the interests they share—salmon fishing and antique collecting among them—and, above all perhaps, a deep love of the open air. The scent of clump grass, the wisp of wind over heath, and the view that extends beyond a person's ability to walk in a day—these are the loves that are in the very blood of both Prince Charles and the Queen Mother.

Above: *From an early age, Prince Charles has always shown a strong love of his grandmother. This picture was taken at Royal Lodge, Windsor*
Below: *A rare picture of both grandmothers. Prince Philip's mother, who died in 1969, is looking down at Princess Anne*

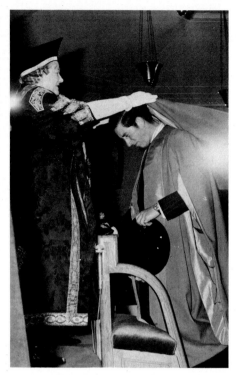

Left: *A proud grandson escorts a proud grandmother to church*

Above: *The Queen Mother conferring an Honorary Degree of Doctor of Laws on her grandson at London University in November 1974*

Below left: *At the Queen Mother's country home, Royal Lodge, Windsor. The picture was taken to mark the Queen Mother's 75th birthday. Prince Andrew's gift was a set of two pottery dishes, which he made himself at Gordonstoun*

Below: *At Ascot in June, 1970, both the Queen Mother and her grandson are elegance personified*

Right: *The official portrait for the Queen Mother's 75th birthday. It was taken in the drawing-room of her London home, Clarence House. Her necklace is of pearl and diamond clusters with linking diamonds*
Below: *Prince Charles and his grandmother sharing a coach during the Queen's Silver Jubilee visit to Scotland*

A sister for the Prince

Prince Charles was one year and nine months old when his sister was born on August 15, 1950, at Clarence House in London—the only one of the Queen and Prince Philip's four children to be born there.

As with his younger brothers when they arrived, Prince Charles had a strong protective feeling towards his only sister almost from the moment she was born. But it was not very long before he—along with others, such as their governess—discovered that Princess Anne had a mind of her own. In nursery squabbles it was occasionally Charles who needed the protection. Whereas the Prince was shy and would withdraw into himself very quickly if his feelings were hurt, the Princess rarely seemed too worried by anyone or anything.

To a certain extent her behaviour was deceptive, for when Charles went away to board at Cheam School his sister is said to have missed him a great deal. But this was partly because she was envious of Charles— she could not wait to get away to school herself.

As teenagers, and during their early twenties, Charles and Anne were like many other brothers and sisters—fond of one another, but aware that their personalities and interests were dissimilar. Princess Anne once remarked: "We live in the same house and have rooms at opposite ends of a corridor. But we usually go out at different times. The only time I see a lot of him is during holidays—and roughly speaking that's enough." The remark may have been somewhat facetious, but it held more than an inkling of truth.

Anne reached the stage of enjoying parties much sooner than Charles. He, in any case, never found the same pleasure in pop music and dancing that his sister did. She had boyfriends before he had girlfriends, and she appeared altogether more at ease in the "Swinging Sixties" than he ever did.

Whether by accident or not, since his sister's wedding in 1973, Prince Charles has

Above: *The first picture of Prince Charles with his sister, taken at Clarence House in September 1950. Princess Anne was born on August 15*

Left: *Brother and sister attend the Garter ceremony at St. George's Chapel, Windsor, in April 1971*

Right: *Anne, already as tall as her brother, arrives at the Braemar Highland Gathering in September 1962*

Far right: *Anne accompanies Charles on his first visit to Wales, in 1960—here they are arriving at Cardiff station*

and to treat him no differently because he was the Queen's son.

He, in turn, did not show signs of thinking of himself in any way special. But he did suffer some disadvantages at first. For instance, his teachers discovered that Charles knew nothing about money, having never handled it. He had never been inside a shop, and until six months after he went to Hill House he had not been on a bus.

He learned to play cricket and enjoyed wrestling. He spent many happy hours drawing and painting, and each Friday afternoon, sitting on a tiny stool, he took tea with the headmaster's wife before the royal chauffeur arrived to take him off to Windsor for the weekend.

Part of his first school report reads as follows:

Lent 1957, Upper VI
READING—*very good indeed. Good expression.*
WRITING—*Good, Firm, Clear, Well-formed.*
ARITHMETIC—*Below form average. Careful but slow—not very keen.*
HISTORY—*Loves this subject.*
SINGING—*A sweet voice, especially in lower register.*

In well-to-do English families of any kind there is a strong tradition of following in father's footsteps, and it came as no real surprise when it was announced that, after two terms at Knightsbridge, Charles would be going to Prince Philip's old preparatory school, Cheam, set among 65 acres on the Berkshire Downs.

Prince Charles has always been a home-loving person, and the thought of going to boarding school made him extremely nervous. The Queen too, like any mother, did not relish the thought of sending her son away to school at the age of eight. She and Prince Philip drove the 60-mile journey from London to see Charles safely into his new school. And after they left, the mathematics master, who had been delegated to keep a special eye on the new arrival, saw a boy "notably in need of a haircut" standing apart from the others and looking very miserable.

Prince Charles quickly recovered from home-sickness, but he was never to be totally happy at Cheam. Though efforts had been made to ensure that he was treated like any other pupil at the school it soon became apparent to the Prince—possibly for the first time—that as heir to the Throne he was in a unique position, forever to be regarded differently from anyone else.

When he was still not 10 he was invited into the headmaster's study one day to watch the Commonwealth Games on television with a few of the other boys. In 1958 the Games took place in Cardiff, but the Queen was prevented from attending because of an attack of sinusitis. However, she had recorded a message which was played to the crowd, and the scene was watched by millions of television viewers. "I intend to create my son, Charles, Prince of Wales, today." Prince Charles flushed with embarrassment as the other boys turned to him with clapping hands and small cheers. "When he is grown up I will present him to you at Caernarvon," the Queen's message continued. Roars of approval rang round the stadium at Cardiff and then the huge crowd took up singing God Bless The Prince of Wales. In Cheam the recipient of their good wishes, watching the cameras range over thousands of anonymous faces, began to realise perhaps just what lay in store for him.

Right: *The school on the Berkshire Downs where Prince Charles went in September 1957, following in his father's footsteps*
Below left: *The Prince respectfully raises his cap to Mr. Beck, the headmaster, on his arrival at the school*
Below: *Back to school—Charles leaves the train at King's Cross station after a holiday in Balmoral*
Oval: *With his governess, Catherine "Mispy" Peebles, travelling to Cheam*
Far right: *On his way to church in July 1958, the day after he was created Prince of Wales*

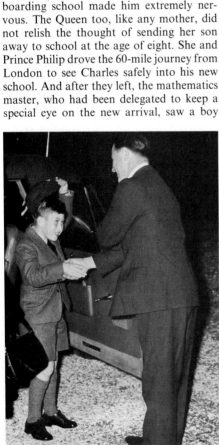

Above: *Following the coronation ceremony, Prince Charles stands next to his mother on the balcony at Buckingham Palace and watches the fly-past of the RAF.* **Left:** *In Westminster Abbey, the Queen Mother listens to her grandson's questions. On his left is Princess Margaret*

A prince at a coronation

By rights, as first royal duke in the land and head of the peerage, Prince Charles, Duke of Cornwall, should have led the way in kissing the hand and swearing allegiance to Queen Elizabeth at her coronation on June 2, 1953. But he was only four, and there was no precedent since the creation of the dukedom in 1337 of a monarch being crowned with a son so young. After some discussion it was decided that the Prince should attend the coronation, or as much of it as he could stand without fidgeting, but should not wear ducal robes, and should not figure in the official list of those present. His little sister, Princess Anne, would stay at home.

For both Charles and Anne the preparations for the coronation were probably as exciting as the event itself. They saw the seamstresses working away at the robes and velvet trains that their mother was to wear. They glimpsed the comings and goings of such great men as Winston Churchill—Prince Charles retains a hazy memory of a large man, a large hat and a large cigar. And, not surprisingly, they were seen once or twice to be dressing up themselves and "playing coronations".

On the great day itself they watched from an upstairs window as their mother and father left Buckingham Palace in the famous Gold State Coach, following a mile-long cavalcade of splendour, marching and trotting towards Westminster Abbey. Then, dressed in a white satin suit, with his hair fussed over and his buckle shoes gleaming, Prince Charles was hurried downstairs by Mrs. Lightbody, the nanny, and taken by car on a roundabout route to Dean's Yard and the Cloisters, and so into the Abbey.

He arrived as the choir was singing Handel's setting of the anthem Zadok The Priest, and it must have mystified him to see his mother not in splendid crimson robes but covered by the plain white garment which she wore for the sacred anointing with oil.

The millions watching on television hardly realised at first that Prince Charles was present. Only when the cameras went into close-up did they see his head and shoulders above the ledge of the royal box where he stood between his grandmother and his aunt, the Queen Mother and Princess Margaret, seemingly firing a barrage of questions.

After half an hour or so it was judged that he had seen enough, and so Mrs. Lightbody took his hand and led him quietly out of a side door and back to the Palace for lunch. When his mother returned, crowned Queen of her realm and a commonwealth beyond, she went, by tradition, on to the balcony to acknowledge the cheering of the masses of well-wishers below. A few moments later the Duke of Edinburgh led the two children out to join her, and Prince Charles looked down, as he was to do so many times again, on a wide sea of faces raising up a great shout of jubilation. Sadly, because he was so young, he can hardly remember it at all.

Below left: *The four-year-old Prince, seemingly becoming bored with the long service*
Below: *A close-up of the Queen and her family at Buckingham Palace after the return from the Abbey*

A mother's influence

In a letter to her former music teacher, Mabel "Goosey" Lander, shortly after Prince Charles was born, the Queen described her baby's hands: "They are rather large, but fine with long fingers—quite unlike mine and certainly unlike his father's. It will be interesting to see what they will become." She added, "I still find it difficult to believe I have a baby of my own!"

The Queen was still Princess Elizabeth when her first child was born, and looking forward to many happy years as a naval officer's wife. The untimely death of King George VI abruptly ended Prince Philip's career in the Royal Navy and might drastically have altered the early lives of both Prince Charles and Princess Anne. But the new Queen Elizabeth would never allow it.

Despite all the official duties which commandeered so much of her time, both she and Prince Philip were determined in setting aside every free moment to give their children as loving an upbringing as possible. The Queen bathed her children and tucked them up in bed. She played with them every morning, from nine to nine-thirty, and if she could snatch any quiet moments during the rest of the day she hurried up to the nursery to be with them.

Both the Queen and Prince Philip had firm ideas about the way they wanted to treat their children, and the way they wanted the children to treat them. Departing from precedent, the Queen and her husband told them when they were five or six that they were not to bow and curtsy to them—though they should do so when they went to see their grandmother.

All through his nursery days the Prince was addressed by everyone simply as Charles, but when he was old enough to understand he was strongly rebuked by his mother for referring to a senior detective and omitting the prefix "Mr." When the Royal children's mother had been a child herself there had seemed little chance she would ever become Queen because at the time she was not in close direct line to the Throne. Her childhood had been carefree, her preparation for royal duties minimal.

But Charles, when he was only three years old, became heir to the Throne, and this had always to be borne in mind. And yet not too much. The Queen always wanted her eldest son to have as normal an upbringing as possible.

She herself had been educated by private tutors, but it was decided that Charles would go to school. He wouldn't be spoiled and he wouldn't be allowed to think that because of his privileged position, he could do more or less whatever he liked.

From an early age he was taught the value of things—once he was sent out to look for a lost dog-lead because, as his mother pointed out, dog-leads cost money. Good manners were insisted upon, lies and deceit were punished.

But most of all the Queen's influence shows in the love her eldest son has always felt for his home and his parents. He really does love his home—and that means his home life, whichever palace it happens to be in. And he has probably never been happier than when his whole family has been together under one roof, at Sandringham or Balmoral, sailing on a loch, picnicking on a hillside.

After he is married none of this is likely to change. There will just be one more person to be included in the family, and eventually another family to start. Prince Charles is lucky that he comes from such a happy, united background, because wealth and position have never, alone, guaranteed these benefits to anyone.

Far left: *This picture was taken at Windsor Castle, a few days before the investiture of the Prince of Wales in 1969*
Oval: *The four-year-old Prince with his mother at Balmoral Castle*
Above: *Mother and son had just been reunited with Prince Philip on his return to London after a three-month tour of the Commonwealth*
Below left: *Another of the posed photographs where Prince Charles, like any other small child, has to be coaxed into staying still for long enough*
Below: *The general public never sees the Royal Family more relaxed than at polo matches. Both Prince Charles and Prince Philip played in this particular game, in 1967*

A father's pride

It is said that when Prince Charles was less than five, his father decreed that, for a while, there should be an end to his son's dancing classes so he could spend more time on boyish, out-of-door activities.

Certainly in the early years Prince Charles was surrounded by women—his nanny, his governess, his nursemaids. After the age of three he had aunts, but no uncles by birth, two grandmothers but no grandfather. And, apart from Earl Mountbatten, his father was not only the main, but almost the only male influence within the inner family circle. No wonder the young Charles showed signs of wanting to emulate him from a remarkably early age, and to prove to him—a much more difficult task—that he was made of the same demanding stuff as his father.

In some ways Prince Philip and Prince Charles are not alike. Charles' sense of humour is much less caustic than his father's—he is inclined to play the fool rather than make another person, intentionally or not, feel a fool. He prefers physical work to being stuck behind a desk, but whatever the situation, both he and his father cannot bear being idle for more than a few minutes.

Prince Philip taught his son to swim and introduced him to the game of polo—at which Charles may be a better horseman, though his father was a more ferocious competitor.

But for Prince Philip's championing, Charles might not have gone to Cheam and then to Gordonstoun, schools whose style of education were less suited to his character than they had been to his father's. But he would be the first to admit how much he benefited from attending both schools, and Philip must have been extremely proud when his son was made guardian (or head boy) of Gordonstoun.

After Charles left school—and then, more important, university (Philip never went to university)—the influence of his father gradually seemed less evident. Or perhaps it was just that Charles' own personality emerged more definitely.

Physically, the two men bear a strong resemblance to one another. And, as everyone knows, they have several mannerisms in common. Charles once told a lunchtime audience that one of the reasons they both walk with their hands behind their backs was that they use the same tailor. (It was a joke that got a laugh, though not everyone understood what he meant!)

Like any father, Prince Philip knows he must leave the stage more and more to his eldest son as both of them grow older. Or rather, they are likely to occupy different parts of the same stage.

Prince Charles has always had tremendous respect for his father, and a love that will probably grow even stronger as the years go by. For his part, Prince Philip must at times reflect on how lucky he has been to have a son who has grown so well into the unique position he holds. Of course, it has by no means been all luck. Prince Charles knows just how much he owes to his father, and the pride is two-way.

Left: *Following the Trooping the Colour ceremony in 1953, father and son stand side by side on the balcony at Buckingham Palace*
Above: *Prince Charles, almost 10, drives with Prince Philip to morning service at Crathie church, near Balmoral*
Below: *Some advice from an expert polo-player to a novice, in 1965. Today Prince Charles is himself a player of international standing. When he played for Young England his father was a keen spectator*

Gordonstoun

44

The choice of Gordonstoun as Prince Charles' next school after Cheam was undoubtedly the first preference of Prince Philip, who had always looked back with pleasure on his own schooldays there. Perhaps his son, with whom alternatives were discussed, might have preferred Charterhouse, in Surrey, if only because his best friend from Cheam was going there. Certainly he found Gordonstoun at first "pretty gruesome". It is said he even wrote to the Queen Mother, asking that he be allowed to transfer somewhere else. But in the tradition of the school, he stuck it out and grew used to early morning runs, ice-cold showers, emptying dustbins, and all the other character-building ploys of the system.

Being in the far north of Scotland, Gordonstoun was at least convenient for half-term holidays at Balmoral, Prince Charles' favourite royal residence. But he never liked Gordonstoun as much as his father had. This might have been partly because the school had grown much bigger, and therefore less intimate, and partly because no son is exactly the same as his father.

Prince Charles liked to prove that he could perform some of the muscle-building activities—such as clambering over the assault course—but he never shared quite the same competitive spirit as Prince Philip, and so javelin-throwing in the early morning never held the same appeal.

He found difficulty in making lasting friendships. Much of the time he went around with three particular boys: his cousin Prince Guelf of Hanover; Norton Knatchbull, another cousin; and Prince Alexander of Yugoslavia.

Perhaps because they were solo activities, Charles took up pottery, and then the cello—hobbies he has since neglected almost entirely. After two years he passed O-level French, history, Latin, English language and literature—he was younger than the others taking the same exams—but mathematics

Oval, far left: *Prince Philip at the age of 16, when he was a pupil at Gordonstoun. Even then, apparently, he held his hands behind his back*

Left: *Captain Iain Tennant, Chairman of the Board of Governors, points out Prince Philip's old classroom to Prince Charles on his first day at Gordonstoun in 1962*

Top: *Meal-time at Gordonstoun. The boy at the head of the table serves out for the others*

Above: *Pupils doing homework in a fairly spartan looking study*

Right: *Father shows son round his old school, on Prince Charles' first day— this picture is somewhat misleading in that Prince Philip is not holding his son's hand*

GORDONSTOUN *continued*

and physics were mountains which he still had to cross.

It was really only when he broke off his time at Gordonstoun to go to school in Australia for two terms that he began to be completely at ease. He returned to Gordonstoun for a further year to take A-level French and history, and to become guardian (head boy) of the school.

Ironically, for one who has managed to avoid any hint of scandal since becoming an adult, it was at Gordonstoun that Prince Charles made headlines around the world, with what became known as the "cherry brandy incident".

Speculation about the episode naturally increased when Buckingham Palace first denied the newspaper reports, then withdrew the denial and confirmed the story.

In fact it all began when the Prince and four other boys from Gordonstoun landed at Stornoway, on the Isle of Lewis, during a sailing expedition on one of the school's ketches. They had permission to lunch at the Crown Hotel and then go to the cinema.

Once Charles was recognised a small crowd gathered and, disliking being peered at through the windows of the hotel lounge, he escaped into the next room, which just happened to be the bar. After hanging around there for a few minutes, with customers watching, he became embarrassed, and so stepped up to the counter and asked for a cherry brandy—the drink he had sometimes been given when out shooting at Sandringham. At almost the same moment a woman journalist entered the bar, recognised the 14-year-old boy, and by the next morning the story had been telegraphed round the world.

For a long time any reference to the incident rankled the Prince, and made him highly suspicious of all journalists. When back at school he was punished—not with the cane, but with demotion to base-level in a training programme. It took him the rest of the term to climb back up again.

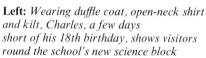

Left: *Wearing duffle coat, open-neck shirt and kilt, Charles, a few days short of his 18th birthday, shows visitors round the school's new science block*
Oval, left: *Meeting his house-master at the start of Charles' first term*
Below left: *A member of the audience, applauding the Queen when she visited the school in 1967*

Above: *Part of the obstacle course at Gordonstoun*
Right: *As guardian (head boy) of the school, Prince Charles shows the Queen around on his last day of school life in July 1967*
Below: *Boys of the third form, in a race over the obstacle course*
Below, right: *Again in the new science block, opened in 1966*

Charlie's aunt

At the christening of Prince Charles at Buckingham Palace in December 1948, it was Princess Margaret who placed the baby in the Archbishop of Canterbury's arms and spoke the four names of her first nephew in a clear steady voice: "Charles Philip Arthur George."

It is said that when she first heard the name that her sister and her brother-in-law intended giving their son, Princess Margaret joked: "I suppose that means I will be called Charlie's aunt." In fact she has always been known within the family as Aunt Margot, and Charles has never been called anything but Charles.

Although, in common with all the Royal Family, Prince Charles had several god-parents, he probably saw more of Princess Margaret in the early years than any of his other god-parents, mainly because she was living just down the road from Buckingham Palace, at Clarence House, with the Queen Mother. But this was also the time, in the early 1950s, when Princess Margaret was burdened with deeply-felt personal problems. Prince Charles was not yet seven when his aunt announced that "mindful of the Church's teaching that Christian marriage is indissoluble" she had decided not to marry Group Captain Peter Townsend, a divorcee with whom she had fallen in love.

Twenty-one years later Princess Margaret and the man she did marry, Lord Snowdon, agreed to a separation, then a divorce.

Prince Charles holds very strong principles and, especially during his middle teens, was a deeply religious person. But it is unlikely that he would have utterly condemned his aunt because, by nature, he is sympathetic to those in trouble and would feel sad rather than sanctimonious about the breakdown of any marriage.

Aunt and nephew are dissimilar in character, but they do share a love of the theatre and the cinema. Perhaps it is fortunate for him that, as heir to the Throne, the course of his life is already more clearly mapped out in advance than Princess Margaret's ever was.

Above: *Waiting with Princess Margaret at London Airport, to meet the Queen and Prince Philip on their return from Canada in 1959*

Left: *Three generations of one family. Princess Margaret was godmother to Prince Charles until his confirmation*

Below left: *At Birkhall, on Deeside, in 1951, where the Queen and Prince Philip spent part of their honeymoon*

Below right: *Arriving for morning service at Crathie church, Balmoral, in August 1962—Princess Margaret's own son, Viscount Linley, was nine months old*

Right: *Princess Margaret takes her nephew's hand as they arrive at Windsor in April 1953, to watch the Queen present new Colours to the Household Cavalry*
Below: *Prince Charles out riding with his aunt in June 1972*

TIMBERTOP continued

Above: *Arriving at Canberra airport, on his way to Timbertop, in January 1966*

Above right: *Ski-ing on the slopes of Mount Buller, 140 miles east of Melbourne, in July*

Below: *At Harley's Creek zoo, Cairns, a dingo puppy was given to the Prince*

Right: *A Honolulu hello and goodbye from an American well-wisher who threw the traditional carnation garland round Prince Charles' shoulders when he stopped off at the island on his way to Timbertop*

Helmet and shield

Strictly speaking, a crest is the device worn on a helmet; a coat of arms is the identification on a shield or on a linen smock worn over armour. Brought together (right) they make up a badge—which the owner can use on almost anything he chooses, from blazer button to cushion cover.

The Prince of Wales' crest—which in the old days would have been made out of carved wood or dried leather—is a crowned lion on top of a crown. His coat of arms embraces signs of England, Scotland, Wales and Ireland.

The ancient Arms of England—three gold lions set against a red background—first appeared on the Great Seal of England, made in about 1195 for Richard the Lionheart. In the 13th century they were called leopards. But then a medieval herald pointed out that the leopard was supposed to have arisen from an adulterous union of lion and cheetah—thought to be hardly suitable parentage for a royal beast—so lions they became from then onwards.

The Arms of Scotland, in the right top quarter of the shield, date from the 13th century. The fleur-de-lys round the edges are held to signify France's ancient protection of Scotland.

In 1603, when James VI of Scotland became James I of England, the union of the two countries was combined on a single shield, and at the same time the Arms of Ireland, a gold harp on a blue background, were added.

Set in the centre of the shield are the Arms of the Principality of Wales, four red and gold lions, dating back to the 13th century and borne by two sons of Llywelyn the Great.

Standing on either side of the royal shield are the gold lion, first used by the Tudors, and the unicorn which came with the union with Scotland. Across the necks of the animals are white bars, or labels, with three points. These show that the arms are those of the eldest son and heir apparent. Other members of the Royal Family have their own distinguishing labels.

Encircling the shield is what looks like a belt but is really a garter signifying membership of the most Noble Order of the Garter, England's highest Order of Chivalry, dating back to 1348.

Worked in along the bottom are the Prince of Wales' feathers, the red dragon of Wales and the Arms of the Duchy of Cornwall.

The legend about the Prince of Wales' ostrich feathers is that the Black Prince plucked them from the blind King of Bohemia on the battlefield of Crécy, but experts now believe it's much more probable they were inherited from his mother, Philippa of Hainault.

There is also some mystery about the origin of the Prince of Wales' motto "Ich

Above: *The Arms of the Prince of Wales*

Right: *An artist's impression of Edward I presenting his baby son to the people of Wales in 1284*

Dien". Some believe the language was not originally German but Welsh, dating from 1284 when Edward I of England, faced with rebellious Welshmen, promised a prince who could speak no word of English. Showing them his son, a few days old, he declared "Eich Dyn"—"Your Man".

The red dragon, on the right, originated from Dacia, north of the Danube, and was subsequently adopted by the Romans as the standard of a cohort. After the Romans left Britain, the dragon remained a symbol of authority for a long time.

Finally, the 15 gold balls in the centre shield. These can be traced back to Richard, Earl of Cornwall and Count of Poitou, the brother of Henry III. They are thought to represent peas or "pois"—which is a pun on the name Poitou.

Places and Titles

Duke of Cornwall

Above: *The picturesque village of Mousehole, Cornwall. Prince Charles has held the title of Duke of Cornwall since birth*

Earl of Chester

Below: *Eastgate, Chester. Prince Charles is Prince of Wales and Earl of Chester, but the titles do not, in fact, bring in any money at all and he owns no estates in either Wales or Cheshire*

Lord of the Isles

Above: *A ruined croft on Raasay, Skye. Among Prince Charles' inherited titles is that of Lord of the Isles and Great Steward of Scotland*

Prince of Wales

Below: *The rough-hewn beauty of Snowdon and Llyn Llydaw. Prince Charles was invested Prince of Wales in 1969, but he derives his income from land and property that make up the Duchy of Cornwall*

A student at Cambridge

Prince Charles was not the first heir to the Throne to go to university. Edward VII went to no less than three—Oxford, Cambridge and Edinburgh. The Duke of Windsor attended Magdalen College, Oxford. And Charles' grandfather, King George VI, went to the same college at Cambridge—Trinity—that Charles himself went up to, almost 50 years later. But unlike his forebears, Charles stayed on to take a degree. And unlike George VI, who lived in a house some distance from the university, he had his own rooms on Staircase E.

He arrived in October 1967 in a red Mini and, he has since written, "All that could be seen in front of Trinity Great Gate were serried ranks of variously trousered legs, from which I had to distinguish those of the Master and the senior tutor . . . Perhaps the most vivid and memorable moment of arrival was when several burly, bowler-hatted gentlemen proceeded to drag shut

Above: *Prince Charles discusses a point with his tutor in a relaxed moment in the college grounds*
Left: *The art of playing the cello attracted Charles, as it had done his ancestor George IV*
Oval: *The Prince had somehow to keep up with his studies and take part in state ceremonies. In the corner of his college living-room, the hi-fi equipment. He loved to listen to classical music*
Far right: *The self-conscious pose of the typical undergraduate. Prince Charles' grandfather, King George VI, also went to Trinity College*

those magnificent wooden gates to prevent the crowd from following in—it was something like a scene from the French Revolution." Someone shouted out: "Good luck". "I'll need it," Charles responded.

He had decided, for the first year at least, to follow up his interest in pre-history and study archaeology and anthropology.

From the start he tried to merge himself among the other students. He cycled to lectures (followed by his detective in a Land-Rover) and wore baggy trousers and a leather-patched sports jacket. But he sometimes felt that the presence of the Queen's eldest son at student parties put a dampener on exuberance, and more and more he associated not with the ex-grammar school boys but with what were termed the "huntin', shootin', and fishin' types".

A group of them including Charles formed a small dining club known as the Wapiti. But even in select circles the Prince knew he had to be careful about what he said, especially in undergraduate political arguments, and how he behaved, especially when high jinks were in the air.

He worked hard at his studies—he was always a diligent student rather than a brilliant one—and the light relief came when he found he could not hide behind his title, but behind the role he was playing on a stage.

It was while he was up at university that the world at large first learned of Charles the comedian. He had taken part in Shakespearean plays at Gordonstoun—playing the Duke of Exeter in Henry V and the title role in Macbeth—but it was after he had been accepted as a member of the Dryden Society at Cambridge that he was able to give freedom to his talent for mimicry and generally playing the fool.

His first stage appearance involved wearing a clerical dog-collar and having a custard pie flung in his face. Then in a two-hour revue of undergraduate sketches, somewhat typically entitled Revu-lution, he dashed about the stage as a Victorian lecher, then stood in a dustbin to make another sort of joke. The whole performance was greatly enjoyed, especially by the best-known name in the cast.

But, on the more serious side, he also played the cello in the college orchestra—classical music rather than jazz or pop music has always been one of his great joys. And on an Easter outing to the Dordogne he spent a few happy days mixing pleasure with study by examining prehistoric cave paintings and joining in an archaeological "dig".

In his second and third years, Prince Charles studied history. But all the while he had had to make room for official duties (including his investiture as Prince of Wales at Caernarvon) and so, as Lord Butler, Master of Trinity once remarked, it was fortunate the Prince had "great powers of concentrating on his work".

In June 1970, despite all the interruptions, "Wales, HRH Prince of" gained a Bachelor of Arts degree in history—Class 2, Division 2, which was not bad at all. And the examiners only looked up the names of the students *after* they had marked the papers. . .

Above: *Prince Charles enjoyed a remarkable degree of privacy at Cambridge. Shopping in the local market, he wasn't subjected to the inquisitive stares of passers-by*

Right: *His rooms in New Court and, in his third year, in Great Court, contained a kitchenette where he could make himself a snack. Prince Charles shares with his mother a simple taste in food. Rice pudding was one of his favourites as a child*

Far right: *The bicycle is the traditional form of transport for undergraduates, but when Prince Charles cycled around Cambridge he had to be followed by his detective—usually riding in a Land-Rover*

The German connection

Most people think of Prince Charles as having only one aunt—his mother's sister, Princess Margaret. But, through marriage, he has two others—Princess Margarita of Hohenlohe-Langenburg and Princess Sophie of Hanover. A third aunt, Princess Theodora of Baden, died in 1969 at the age of 63. Her sister, Princess Cecilie, was killed in an air crash, in 1937, at the age of 26.

All four women grew up as the elder sisters of Prince Philip—the oldest was 16 years older than her only brother and Sophie, the youngest, was born seven years before Philip.

All five children belonged to Prince Andrew of Greece and his wife Princess Alice of Battenberg, who died in 1969—she was a sister of Lord Louis Mountbatten.

Each of Prince Philip's sisters married a member of the German aristocracy, and at the end of World War II, when Prince Philip was courting the heir to the British Throne, the fact that there was this "German connection" worried some establishment figures in England. But it turned out that both Prince Philip and Princess Elizabeth were so popular that the great majority were unconcerned about whom Prince Philip's sisters had married.

Whether or not it is as part of a deliberate policy, Prince Charles' relations on his father's side have seldom figured in the welter of publicity constantly surrounding the Royal Family. Unknown to most people, Charles' paternal grandmother spent the last three years of her life, almost a complete invalid, in Buckingham Palace. She occupied the Buhl Suite, where her grandson was born, and where she died at the age of 84.

Altogether, Prince Philip's four sisters gave birth to 19 children—giving Prince Charles a great many cousins by marriage. Princess Sophie has the largest family—two princes and three princesses by her first marriage to Prince Christopher of Hesse, and two princes and one princess by her second marriage to Prince George of Hanover. Her third son, the late Prince Welf, born in 1947, was a fellow-pupil of Prince Charles at Gordonstoun.

When they were still children, Charles and Anne accompanied their father fairly frequently on visits to their German relatives. More recently, when members of the Royal Family pay official visits to the Continent they will sometimes stay on afterwards for private calls on one or more of their numerous relations.

Above: *Queen Victoria's parents. Her mother was Princess Victoria of Leiningen, Bavaria; her father, fourth son of George III*

Left: *Queen Victoria with her husband, who was Duke of Saxony and Prince of Saxe-Coburg and Gotha, before he became Prince Consort*

Above: *Prince Philip with his sister, Princess Theodora of Baden, in 1965.* **Right:** *In 1969 Prince Charles flies to the Continent for the funeral of Princess Theodora*

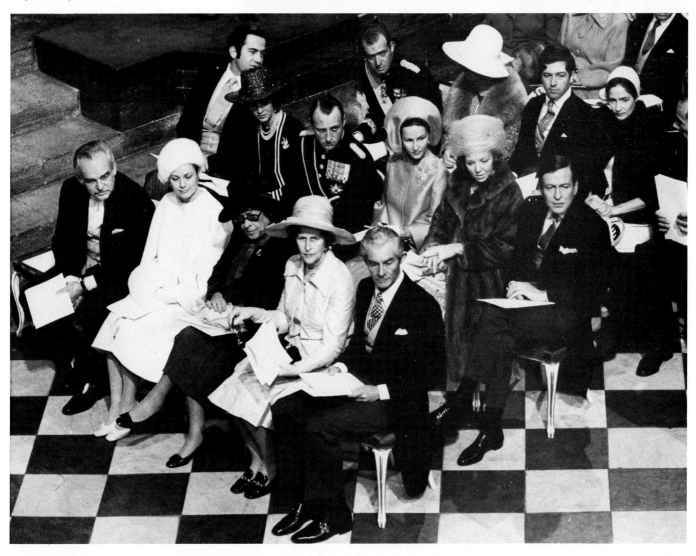

Above: *In the front row at Princess Anne's wedding in 1973, next to Prince Rainier and Princess Grace, are Princess Margarita of Hohenlohe-Langenburg and Princess Sophie and her second husband, Prince George of Hanover*

Myfyriwr yn Aberystwyth

A student in Aberystwyth

Left: *On the first day of his nine-week course at the University College of Wales*
Right: *On top of Snowdon, the highest mountain in Wales. The Prince made the climb with the Countryside in 1970 Committee for Wales, of which he was Chairman. Many of the other members were still plodding to the top while he was already on the way down*
Below: *Scenes from his stay at Aberystwyth, including a picture of him at work in the language laboratory. Learning the Welsh language was part of the preparation for his investiture as Prince of Wales*

Taking a course in the Welsh language at a Welsh university would seem a fairly natural thing for a Prince of Wales to do. But when the idea was publicly mooted it met with feverish opposition from a minority of the Welsh people, mainly students. There was a sit-in, and a hunger-strike by seven, and the National Union of Students criticised the idea of a course lasting only one term. Generally, the feeling of the opposition seemed to be that, as Charles was not Welsh, the whole exercise was something of a sham.

Characteristically, the Prince of Wales replied to his critics by displaying both a sense of humour and a sense of purpose.

From the day he was formally enrolled for a nine-week term at University College of Wales, Aberystwyth—April 21, 1969, his mother's 43rd birthday—he applied himself to five hours a day in the language laboratory. In less than six weeks he made his first public speech in Welsh to a League of Youth National Eisteddfod numbering around 5,000. His pronunciation was judged excellent, but he did most to silence his critics when he declared his loyalty to the Welsh language: "Having spent so many hours in the language laboratory I shall never let it die without offering stout resistance . . ."

On another occasion he told of how the Mayor of Llanelli had asked him to pronounce the name of the town. "I said Llanelli and the mayor wiped the saliva out of his eye and said 'Well done'".

Welsh nationalism was probably no less fervent after Prince Charles left Aberystwyth to finish his studies at Cambridge. But there must have been quite a few among the opposition to his visit who had found that, as one student put it, "he's quite an amiable chap with a lively sense of humour."

Linked with his name

Prince Charles was barely 10 years old when a Sunday newspaper came out with a guess-list of names of girls—all of them, like him, still children—any one of whom could be considered a possible future bride for the heir to the Throne. (Sadly for the newspaper's reputation as an accurate forecaster of news, the name of the lady he is in fact going to marry did not figure on the list of six.)

Since then, hardly a month has gone by without someone somewhere publishing a picture and asking the question: Is this the girl Charles is going to marry? The public was naturally curious. After all, the Prince of Wales is, or rather was, the world's most eligible bachelor. And, as he himself pointed out in an interview in 1975: "There is bound to be interest in the topic—for a start, a Prince of Wales hasn't been married since 1863."

The first girl in his life, as one newspaper put it, was Rosaleen Bagge, the daughter of a

Above: *Hands across the roof—Prince Charles greets a friend in the car park at a polo match. Photographers know from long experience that the best chance of getting informal shots like this occur when the Prince is getting ready to play polo*

Oval: *At almost exactly the same spot—Smith's Lawn, Windsor—some 20 years earlier*

Left: *Carriage driving, with Davina Sheffield at his side*

Above: *Meeting Princess Caroline of Monaco, in 1977*

Norfolk landowner, whom he met at a dance while he was still a schoolboy and on holiday at Sandringham.

After he went on an exchange visit to Timbertop, his Australian school, she wrote him a letter, and he wrote back. Further correspondence made them friends but, alas for the gossip columnists, no more. Now, like so many of Charles' so-called girl-friends, Rosaleen is married.

Then there was Sibella Dorman, a fellow-student at Cambridge whose father was Governor General of Malta. In 1969, after his investiture as Prince of Wales, Charles went to stay with the family for a week and he and Sibella swam and sunbathed together. A year later he returned for another Maltese holiday. But Sibella is also now married.

During a television interview in 1969 the 20-year-old Prince Charles spoke for the first time, in public at least, about his thoughts on marriage. "You have got to remember that when you marry in my position you are going to marry somebody who perhaps one day is going to become Queen.

"You have got to choose somebody very carefully, I think, who could fulfil this particular role, and it has got to be somebody pretty special.

"The one advantage about marrying a princess, for instance, or somebody from a royal family, is that they do know what happens.

"The only trouble is that I often feel I would like to marry somebody English. Or perhaps Welsh. Well, British anyway."

With these views as a guideline, the tendency thereafter was to divide the Prince's companions into those who could be considered as girlfriends and those who were potentially his bride-to-be. The only problem was, there were so few princesses in Europe of a similar age to the Prince, and so few occasions when he was seen in their company.

So the guessing game went on. There was Lucinda Buxton, daughter of Prince Philip's friend Aubrey Buxton, the naturalist. And Lady Leonora Grosvenor, elder daughter of the Duke of Westminster. Lady Rose Nevill, third daughter of the Marquess and Marchioness of Abergavenny, and Anna Wallace, daughter of wealthy landowner Hamish Wallace.

Then, of course, there was Lady Charlotte Curzon, youngest of Earl Howe's daughters, and Lucia Santa Cruz, daughter of a Chilean diplomat. There was Laura Jo Watkins, daughter of an American rear-admiral, and Davina Sheffield, daughter of an army major.

And most of all, perhaps—because for a long time she was many people's secret bet as the one who *would* be princess—there was Lady Jane Wellesley, daughter of the Duke of Wellington.

In 1975, in an interview for Woman's Own, Prince Charles admitted: "I've fallen in love with all sorts of girls, but I've made sure I haven't married the first person I've fallen in love with . . . Marriage is a much more important business than just falling in love."

Rosaleen Bagge— she and Prince Charles corresponded when he was at school in Australia

Sibella Dorman, a fellow-student at Cambridge—he visited her home in Malta

Lucinda Buxton, daughter of Aubrey Buxton, a keen naturalist, whose home is near Sandringham

Lady Rose Nevill, daughter of the Marquess and Marchioness of Abergavenny, who are close friends of the Royal Family

Anna Wallace, debutante daughter of the wealthy landowner Hamish Wallace

Lucia Santa Cruz, daughter of the former Chilean Ambassador to Britain

Laura Jo Watkins, an American admiral's daughter whom Prince Charles met at a Californian cocktail party

Lady Jane Wellesley, daughter of the Duke of Wellington and a long-standing friend of the Prince

Lady Sarah Spencer, Lady Diana's elder sister, a popular companion at polo and ski-ing in 1978

Set for take-off

According to his instructors, Prince Charles would have made an excellent fighter-pilot. After his first solo flight he remarked that once he was in the air he felt absolutely marvellous

Prince Charles learned to fly mostly while he was up at Cambridge, cramming the lessons between university lectures. He flew solo for the first time in January 1969 after 14 hours' instruction, commenting, "I only had time for a few butterflies in the tummy. The moment I was in the air it was absolutely marvellous."

Two years later he entered the RAF and spent most of the spring and summer learning to fly jet aircraft. The operation was somewhat grandly code-named "Golden Eagle"—not by the Prince!—and involved operational experience on bombers and anti-submarine patrols as well as piloting trainer fighters. This was a considerable achievement, especially for someone who had always had trouble with maths, because a high standard of maths is needed in navigational flying.

But Charles was not prepared to leave it there. Although making a parachute jump was not an obligatory part of his course at RAF College, Cranwell, he decided he would like to have a go. "I'm stupid enough to keep trying things," he said later. He also believes he has constantly to prove himself. "Perhaps I push myself too much. But this is my outlook on life."

The jump, in 1971, was made on a perfect summer's day, into the English Channel off Poole in Dorset. Two officers went first, to give an indication of wind direction and drift, and then it was Charles' turn to step out into air at a height of 1,200 feet.

Despite the taking of all "reasonable precautions", the Prince managed to get his feet caught in the parachute rigging but fortunately they weren't tangled. "A hairy experience," he conceded later.

Another "sometimes bloody terrifying" experience was learning to fly helicopters, which he undertook while he was in the Royal Navy.

In September 1974 he was posted to the Royal Naval Air Station at Yeovilton in Somerset, and after his first flight in a Wessex Mark 5 commando helicopter his instructor described him as a "natural". After 53 hours' ground instruction and 15 hours' solo flying he passed out as the best pilot on the course, and went on to join 845 Naval Air Squadron in the commando ship Hermes. He made many landings and take-offs on the aircraft carrier in a helicopter, but never as pilot of a jet—an ambition which was thought inadvisable for an heir to the Throne. But in 1977, the Prince did at least get the chance to fly as passenger in a jet taking off from a carrier.

Undoubtedly Prince Charles has a natural aptitude for flying, as his passing out report stated. It also suggested he "will make an excellent fighter pilot at supersonic speeds".

Today, while not flying quite as fast as sound, Prince Charles makes great use of the Queen's Flight, piloting himself around the country in almost the same way as others make use of a car.

PRINCE CHARLES' INVESTITURE *continued*

for the occasion consisting of white satin breeches, a mantle and a surcoat of purple edged with ermine, I decided that things had gone too far . . . What would my Navy friends say if they saw me in this preposterous rig?"

Prince Charles was spared—or perhaps, could insist on being spared—such embarrassment. He would wear his ceremonial uniform as Colonel-in-Chief of the Royal Regiment of Wales. Lord Snowdon on the other hand, always the jaunty one, designed for himself a barathea tunic and trousers in dark hunting-green, with a black silk tasselled belt. Rather unkindly, it earned him the nickname "Buttons".

Some 4,000 people were invited to witness the ceremony from inside the Castle grounds, but an estimated 50,000 crowded into Caernarvon itself—nearly five times the town's normal population. Millions more around the world had a close-up view on their television screens. Among the viewers was the Duke of Windsor in Paris.

Lord Snowdon and his small team of designers had produced a background for a rich but unornate spectacle. In the strong likelihood that the Welsh clouds would drench the whole affair, he had designed a see-through canopy that would keep the royal party dry and would allow everyone else a clear view of all that went on—even though they themselves might get wet. The

acrylic canopy and the standards that hung from the ancient walls had been tested for wind resistance. Turf had been imported to cover the stone slabs of the courtyard, and sombre grey slate had been used for the simple thrones and dais.

Against the overcast afternoon of July 1, the colours combined well, especially with the red of the uniforms and the greens and blues of ladies' coats.

Prince Charles, as was befitting, was the first principal to arrive at the Castle. To a fanfare of trumpets he was conducted to the Chamberlain Tower, there to await the summons from the Queen. When Her Majesty arrived at the Water Gate of the Castle she had first to demand entry, in time-honoured tradition, and receive and surrender back the key—15 inches long and weighing $6\frac{1}{2}$ lb.—from Lord Snowdon.

Then after Prince Charles had been brought from the Tower, accompanied by Lords carrying the insignia of a Prince of Wales—rod, mantle, ring, sword and coronet—the Letters Patent, or proof of authority, were read both in English and Welsh.

Charles knelt before the Queen, his mother, and she placed a coronet of gold and diamonds on his head and laid a mantle of ermine across his shoulders. To the millions of people watching in their homes, this was

Above: *The Queen presents her son to the people of Wales at Queen Eleanor's Gate. In the foreground, a statue of David Lloyd George, driving force behind the investiture of the Prince of Wales in 1911*
Below: *The Queen kisses her son after he has pledged his loyalty*
Right: *The ceremony over, the Prince of Wales leaves to drive through Caernarvon*

Left: *The formal picture for posterity—the Prince of Wales wearing the ermine cloak, the sword, and the coronet*

Above: *Following the investiture ceremony on July 1, 1969, Prince Charles*

toured the Principality of Wales. Here he is with the Mayor of Swansea at the time

Below: *Driving around Carmarthen Park, to the cheers of children*

one of the most moving moments in the ceremony.

Then he, still kneeling, put his hands between those of his mother and proclaimed: "I, Charles Prince of Wales, do become your liege man of life and limb and of earthly worship, and faith and truth I will bear unto you to live and die against all manner of folks."

After the reading of the Loyal Address and the saying of prayers there came the moment for the Queen formally to present her son to the people of Wales. Taking his hand and holding it high, she went first to Queen Eleanor's Gate where the mass of people in the street below cheered their loyal good wishes. Then to the King's Gate, and on to the Lower Ward where the presentation was just as popular.

In all, the ceremony lasted hardly an hour. And some thought it archaic, others a waste of money. But by far the majority saw it as meaningful pageantry, stirring to witness, a memory to enjoy. The only tragedy, connected with the event, was that two men blew themselves up with a home-made bomb and an 11-year-old boy stepped on a bomb just outside the Castle and lost a leg in the explosion. The Prince made a donation, later in the year, to the Mayor of Caernarvon's appeal fund for the boy.

After the investiture Prince Charles went on to tour Wales and received welcome and homage from thousands of well-wishers.

The changing face . . .

Travelling man

Above: *A drive-around at Invercargill, the southernmost city of New Zealand*

Below: *In the same town, Prince Charles and Princess Anne were asked to view the prizewinning Hereford bull*

In the spring of 1970, while his fellow-students at Cambridge were using the vacation to swot up for their exams, Prince Charles took off for New Zealand to join his parents and Princess Anne on their royal tour of the Pacific. It was the start of an eight-month period when he was to cover more miles in overseas tours than he had altogether previously. Before Christmas came round he went to New Zealand, Australia, Japan, Canada, America, Fiji, Bermuda and Barbados. And in between he sat *and* passed his finals at Cambridge.

In Auckland, New Zealand, Charles tried square-dancing at the local YMCA and at Hobart, Tasmania, he was told by Sister Gabrielle, in charge of pupils from a convent: "You're my favourite bloke—and that goes for the girls too." Throughout the tour the crowds of spectators were to appreciate for the first time that the Prince of Wales, whom they'd previously thought of as a diffident schoolboy, was now a confident and handsome young man.

In Australia he went surfing at Bondi Beach and the quieter Coogee Beach, and the pin-up pictures of the bare-chested Prince went winging round the world's newspapers.

Speculation that Prince Charles would one day become Governor General of Australia has fluctuated over the years, but there is no doubt that he does genuinely have a special affection for the country. In April 1970 he told young farmers at a Melbourne lunch: "By the greatest good fortune you happen to live in Australia today—good fortune because I believe it is one of the best places anyone can live. I spent six months in this country in 1966 and will never forget it. Australia came to mean a great deal to me, so much so that whenever I come back I experience a curious and inexplicable sense of feeling I belong and it is in fact home."

From Australia Charles made a 14-hour flight to Tokyo—"I don't know why I am the only one who gets all the long flights," he complained, not too seriously—and within the next few hours had attended two receptions and formally dined with the Emperor of Japan. His visit was not official, but it was the first important overseas trip he had made on his own, and it almost certainly paved the way for the Queen and Prince Philip's state visit to Japan in 1975. "Charming, easy-going, tactful" were the epithets he earned after touring 21 pavilions of the international Expo '70 exhibition. And when the head of one of Japan's largest electronics firms talked of plans to build a factory in Europe, the Prince quickly outlined the advantages of Wales. Happily, four years later, the firm did in fact open a new factory in Glamorgan.

In July, 1970, with the relief of knowing he had gained his university degree, Prince Charles flew out to Canada for a 10-day visit with the Queen and Prince Philip, which was followed by a three-day trip with Princess

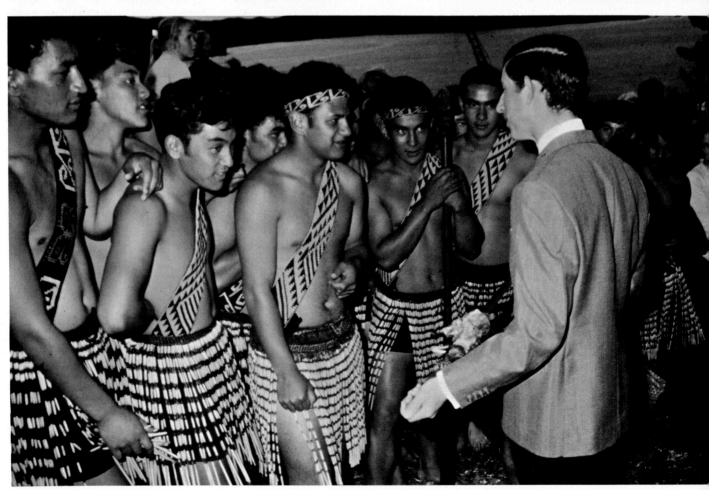

Left: *Rows of broad grins and panama hats welcome Prince Charles to the school-children's gathering at the Hutt Recreation Reserve near Wellington—one of the most relaxed parts of the 1970 tour of New Zealand*
Below left: *Friendly Maori "warriors" chat with the Prince at Mercury Bay*
Above: *In New Zealand, Prince Charles talks to one of the young life-savers who patrol the beaches*
Below: *With the emphasis on informality, the 1970 tour included several highly-popular walkabouts in the towns and cities of Australia and New Zealand*
Below right: *A weekend on a sheep farm at Mount Peel gave Charles a brief opportunity to leave behind the official engagements and sample the country life of New Zealand*

Anne when they travelled south to Washington and visited the White House of President Nixon.

This was in the pre-Watergate halcyon period when the Nixon sisters, Tricia and Julie, and Julie's husband, David Eisenhower, could join with the Queen's children in a kind of Anglo-American family party. There was a baseball game, a barbecue and a ball to which Charles escorted Tricia. President Nixon had the Prince along to his Oval Office for a 20-minute chat that lasted, to Charles' "amazed embarrassment" an hour-and-a-half, and most Americans probably went along with a reporter's description of the Queen's son as charming, sexy and adroit. "If he weren't in line to be King of England he might be able to catch on fast in politics over here."

One hundred and ninety-four years separated Prince Charles' visit to America and that country's independence from his ancestor George III.

Ninety-six years of British rule ended in Fiji in October of the same year when the Prince attended the week-long independence celebrations. He was shown the preparations for the feast—14,000 potatoes, 119 pigs and 23 turtles. And as he saw the live turtles lying on their backs and obviously suffocating in the heat, he had a quiet word with a Fijian minister so that water was poured on to the unfortunate animals.

Then, watched by some 30,000 cheering onlookers, he drank a draught of the local drink, offered in traditional welcome and supposedly prepared by village virgins who chew the root of a shrub called Piper Methysticum and then spit into a ceremonial bowl of water . . .

Up and away next to Bermuda, on the other side of the American continent, stopping off for the night at Acapulco as the guest of actress Merle Oberon and her husband, old friends of Prince Philip.

The Prince's main duty in Bermuda was to open the 350th session of Britain's oldest colonial Parliament. But racial tensions and anti-Monarchist feelings had been growing among the black population, so everything was planned on a low key. Reading the speech from the throne in Parliament, Prince Charles nonetheless made the point: "No society can live and prosper under recurrent acts and threats of violence and such threats—and problems which give rise to them—must be eliminated and law and order maintained."

Twelve members of the Progressive Labour Party boycotted the Prince's two-day visit, but when he left Bermuda for Barbados the island's newspaper, the Royal Gazette, paid him a tribute as "the Prince who stole a thousand hearts".

In Barbados, too, Charles met with at least one manifestation of the Black Power movement. The President of the Students Union stood, with right fist clenched, then grabbed the Prince's hand, palms across. "Do you always stand like that?" asked the slightly bemused visitor.

But while exploring a shopping centre, after a morning of diving and water-skiing, he was almost overwhelmed by girls who rushed from a nylon factory shouting, "You are great, Prince. You are beautiful."

Altogether 1970 was an eventful year for the Prince of Wales—a mixture of sun and sand, and a wider experience of a world where attitudes are always changing. His foreign travels ended that year when, in November, he represented the Queen at the memorial service for General de Gaulle in Paris—a fresh-faced young man among the ageing prime ministers and presidents, performing the kind of onerous and sad duty that will fall to him many more times in the coming years.

Left: *Striding between pavilions at Expo '70, the international exhibition in Tokyo*
Above: *In the grounds of Togu Palace, Tokyo, with the Crown Prince and Princess of Japan and their four-year-old second son*
Below left: *Receiving a souvenir book from two Japanese girls employed at the British Embassy in Tokyo. While Prince Charles was visiting Japan, his parents and sister were on a tour of Australia*
Below: *In the Russian Pavilion at Expo '70 Prince Charles is shown a panoramic model of the super-modern Tashkent City*
Right: *Prince Charles and Princess Anne were the guests of President Nixon's daughters on a three-day visit to America in July 1970. On Princess Anne's left are Tricia Nixon, Julie and Julie's husband David Eisenhower*

Above: *Prince Charles and President Nixon's daughter Tricia pore over a programme before watching a game of baseball—a game which is as baffling to most Britons as polo is to most Americans*
Below: *Tricia Nixon and her sister Julie, married to David Eisenhower, showed Prince Charles and Princess Anne around Washington during their three-day visit in July 1970*
Right: *Outside the White House President Nixon, looking towards his wife, formally welcomes Prince Charles and Princess Anne to Washington*

Above: *On the balcony of the White House with the ill-fated Richard Nixon*
Right: *On arrival at Andrews Air Force Base, near Washington, Princess Anne has a word with welcoming Americans*
Below: *A 22-year-old Prince Charles leaves London for Paris to represent the Queen at the memorial service for President de Gaulle*
Below right: *Among the ageing crowned heads of Europe and Africa, a youthful Prince Charles stands behind the soon-to-be deposed Emperor Haile Selassie of Ethiopia at the memorial service to General de Gaulle in November 1970*

Sailor ahoy!

There was never much doubt that, like his father, his grandfather and his great-grandfather, Prince Charles would enter the Royal Navy. Tradition apart, he had spent hours as a child being taught to sail by his father, and in taking part in fairly tough boating adventures at Gordonstoun. The sea was in his blood.

"The Navy I think means a great deal to me," he once said, "because I was basically brought up on it." Then he added: "I had a very glamorous romantic idea about it which isn't always borne out because there are an awful lot of mundane tasks."

Altogether Charles served five years in the Senior Service, joining as an acting sub-lieutenant in September 1971 and undergoing a six-week graduate course at the Royal Naval College at Dartmouth—where, incidentally, over 20 years earlier, the Queen first met Prince Philip when he was a cadet and she was a visiting teenage princess.

His pay was £4·40 a day (minus £1 a day for food and board), which in fact he signed over to the King George's Fund for Sailors. And his motive was well-expressed when he referred in a speech to a minority of critics: "It is pointless and ill-informed to say that I am entering a profession trained in killing . . . The services are there for fast, efficient and well-trained action in defence. Surely the services must attract a large number of duty-conscious people? Otherwise who else would subject themselves to being square-bashed, shouted at by petty officers and made to do ghastly things in force 10 gales? . . . To me it is a worthwhile occupation and one which I am convinced will stand me in good stead for the rest of my life."

Prince Philip had once said: "Going to sea is not purely a military operation, it is a professional one. Altogether you live in a highly technological atmosphere, probably a good introduction to the kind of thing which controls our whole existence. And aboard ship you learn to live with people, that is the important thing."

After Dartmouth—where his great-uncle, the late Lord Mountbatten, was proud to say Prince Charles had come "top in navigation and top in seamanship, and that is all we seamen care about"—Charles flew out to Gibraltar to join the guided missile destroyer Norfolk, and to work towards his watch-keeping certificate and certificate of naval competence. To most of his fellow-officers he was known simply as "Wales".

After nine months with Norfolk and more training on shore establishments—including being air-locked into the bottom of a 60-ft. water tower for submarine escape drill—he served a year-and-a-half aboard Minerva and then Jupiter, two of Her Majesty's frigates. These 18 months included some of the sunniest times in his life, taking him all over the world.

Prince Charles was 27 when he took command of his first ship—two years younger than Prince Philip had been when he was made captain of HMS Magpie more

Above: *Shouting his orders from the bridge, the captain of HMS Bronington, the Prince of Wales. The 360-ton mine-hunter was leaving the Pool of London in November 1976 and heading back to base at Rosyth*

Below: *As a 15-year-old sea cadet, Prince Charles (directly behind the sailor in the white polo-neck sweater) took part in a seven-day course at Portsmouth with other boys from Gordonstoun*

Speeding to shore, with his pennant at the prow

Oval: *Royal salute from the captain*

SAILOR AHOY! *continued*

than 25 years before. In February 1976 he journeyed to Scotland to go aboard HMS Bronington in Rosyth dockyard. Bronington was a 360-ton mine-hunter, built of wood and 20 years old. She had a company of four officers and 33 ratings, and the captain's cabin measured eight feet by six.

She had a reputation for rolling badly even in moderate weather, and Prince Charles later confessed that the Bronington was the only ship that made him sea-sick.

For nine months he commanded his little ship in a number of British and Nato exercises and "showed the flag" in many British, German and Belgian ports. He also managed, like any good sailor, to have a highly enjoyable time whenever he was ashore, going to parties and even organising—in his last month—a two-and-a-half-hour variety show for the benefit of his crew and the rest of the Royal Navy stationed at Rosyth.

Prince Andrew, on holiday from Gordonstoun, visited his brother in November 1976 and was taken along on a naval exercise at sea. A few days later Prince Charles welcomed his parents aboard when Bronington berthed at London's Tower Pier, a very proud moment for all of them.

The following month Prince Charles—after completing his five years—left the Royal Navy "to do other things", as he put it. One of the major tasks lying ahead was the launching of the Queen's Silver Jubilee Appeal. However, his departure from the Navy did not herald, as some predicted, an early announcement of his engagement. . .

Below: *Prince Charles, sporting the start of a beard, about to climb into a helicopter. The picture comes from the BBC film Pilot Royal, first shown in 1975. Charles was on a commando training course in Canada*

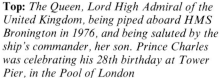

Top: *The Queen, Lord High Admiral of the United Kingdom, being piped aboard HMS Bronington in 1976, and being saluted by the ship's commander, her son. Prince Charles was celebrating his 28th birthday at Tower Pier, in the Pool of London*

Above: *Serving as a lieutenant on the frigate Minerva. The ship was about to leave Devonport in February 1973 for the sunnier Caribbean*

Left: *An unrecognisable Prince Charles surfacing in the submarine-escape training tank at Gosport from a depth of 60 feet*

Above right: *The captain of his ship— Charles on the bridge of Bronington during a naval exercise in the Firth of Forth*

Right: *Acting Sub-Lieutenant the Prince of Wales at his "passing-out" day parade at the Royal Naval College, Dartmouth, October 1971*

Above: *Admiral of the Fleet, the Duke of Edinburgh, calls on his son's ship at Rosyth*

Below: *Using aircraft control "bats" aboard HMS Jupiter at Devonport in April 1974*

Girl of the '80s

Any lunch hour you could take a walk anywhere within a square mile of Sloane Square—which is socially as well as geographically about halfway between Mayfair and Fulham—and within a minute you could expect to see a score of young women who dressed and looked much as Lady Diana did up until her engagement day.

There is a combination of the gamine and the county in those girls who go to English boarding schools and who come to live in London that is instantly recognisable.

Notwithstanding, Lady Diana has her own individual style, which is very much that of an '80s girl. Casual, comfortable, aware of fashion, but not a slave to it. But certainly she can be adventurous, as was shown by the stunning, strapless taffeta gown she wore on her first public engagement with Prince Charles in March 1981.

No doubt her taste will show a change in the coming months, but up until now Lady Diana has favoured lambswool V-necked

sweaters and pleated skirts, soft Liberty print shirts and high-necked Edwardian style blouses, and close-fitting Falmers jeans. She is tall—about 5 ft 9 in.—so she is lucky that the current fashion is for "flattie" shoes. In high heels she would look quite a bit taller than Prince Charles.

It is said that before she and her fiancé bought her engagement ring from Garrard's —a beautiful oval sapphire surrounded by 14 diamonds and set in 18 carat white gold, price £28,500—Lady Diana's jewel case contained only a gold chain bracelet, a necklace and a pair of ear-rings. Hard to believe it was *so* limited, but like most young women of her age she tends to prefer chunky watches and "fun" jewellery to pearls and twin sets.

Or, at least, she has up to now. No doubt, in a short while, the fashion to follow will not be the "Lady Di look", but the Princess of Wales style.

And that is likely to be *quite* different.

It seems only yesterday that Lady Diana Spencer was, by no means nobody, but known to the world at large mainly as the latest to be named in the gossip columns as Prince Charles' newest girlfriend. It seems only yesterday, too, that she was one of the many aristocratic-looking young ladies living in Knightsbridge or South Kensington who have long been known as "The Sloane Rangers".

But Lady Diana always had a style of her own— for one thing, she was too much of an individualist merely to follow the latest trend. Perhaps the letter "D" on the gold chain (above) had many counterparts. But

*not every '80s girl would be brave enough to wear corduroy culottes one day and happy to wear flatties, a skirt and jumper the next. The engagement ring (**left**), admittedly, could never be exactly emulated . . .*

Above and right: *The Lady Diana who went to work (note the black-spotted tights) and who looked stunning with her coat collar turned up, or her cardigan thrown over her shoulders—pictures taken before her engagement when she was trying to lead a normal life . . .*

Country Life

One of the best-kept Royal secrets of 1980 was Prince Charles' interest in, and eventual purchase of a Georgian mansion in Gloucestershire that was ideal for a wealthy couple wanting to set up home in the country and start a family.

Highgrove House, a mile south of Tetbury, in the tiny hamlet of Doughton (pronounced Duffton), had belonged to Maurice Macmillan, M.P., son of the former Conservative Prime Minister, Harold Macmillan, since 1965. The purchase price then was £89,000. Fifteen years later, Prince Charles paid something over £750,000 for the privilege of owning a Georgian mansion with 30 rooms and 347 acres of land.

David Hicks, the late Earl Mountbatten's son-in-law, who designed the interiors of Gatcombe Park and the Prince's private rooms in Buckingham Palace, supervised the extensive redecoration and renovation that was necessary before the new occupant of Highgrove could move in.

Many people wondered at the time why Prince Charles had decided to make his home in Gloucestershire when he already had the free use of Chevening, a fine 17th-century mansion near Chipstead, Kent.

This house, designed by Inigo Jones, had been bequeathed to the nation in 1967 by the 7th Earl of Stanhope, a former Cabinet minister, with the express wish that Prince Charles should be the one to live there and enjoy its 3,500 acres of parkland and profitable farms.

However, by 1973 there was still no official news of what was to be the final outcome. A Buckingham Palace spokesman stated that Prince Charles would definitely not take it. But then, in the following May, the Prime Minister announced that the heir to the Throne would, after all, move into Chevening as soon as renovation and refurbishing had been completed.

The house, with its many finely-proportioned rooms, library, beautiful staircase of Spanish oak and fully modernised bathrooms and kitchen, was clearly intended to become a first home for a newly-married Prince and his wife.

But apparently Prince Charles never had a genuine warmth for the place. It was, perhaps, too grand, too large, and above all too far away from his beloved polo grounds and not too easy, either, to drive to and from Buckingham Palace.

It is said that it was Princess Anne who tipped off her elder brother that Highgrove was about to come on to the market. Visiting her home, at Gatcombe Park, only eight miles away from Highgrove, Prince Charles was undoubtedly impressed by the speed with which he could drive down the motorway from London, and conscious of the fact that this was Beaufort Hunt country and Cirencester Park was handy for polo.

A family man by nature and a lover of Georgian architecture by inclination, Highgrove appealed to the Prince in a way that Chevening never had. He has often remarked to tenants of his farms in the Duchy of Cornwall that he would like to take up farming himself—the Queen and Prince Philip have always taken a keen interest in the management of the Queen's estates at Sandringham and Balmoral. And their eldest son has always had a soft spot for the image of his ancestor George III, popularly known as Farmer George.

Country houses and family farms—the idea appeals, and apparently not only to Prince Charles.

Only a few months after the Royal Prince acquired Highgrove, his cousin Prince Michael of Kent, bought a £300,000 Queen Anne manor house at Nether Lypiatt, only a few miles away. The Prince and Princess Michael moved into their new home in the spring of 1981.

Balmoral and Sandringham will always hold a very special place in the hearts of the Royal Family, but perhaps Princess Anne, then Prince Charles, and now Prince Michael have established a new tradition. Where they all live is already being called The Royal Cotswolds.

Above: *Nether Lypiatt, near Stroud, is the home of the latest Royal residents of the Cotswolds—Prince and Princess Michael of Kent—who moved there in spring 1981*

Left: *Prince Charles was never very happy with the choice of his first private home—Chevening in Kent*

Right, above: *Although not a particularly fine example of Georgian architecture, Highgrove stands amidst acres of beautiful parkland*

Right: *Gatcombe Park, where Princess Anne lives, is only eight miles from Prince Charles' new home*

Above: *Making a point to Lady Sarah Spencer, Lady Diana's sister, at an international polo match at Windsor*
Left: *The parade before the Wills International Polo Match at Smith's Lawn, Windsor, in July 1977*
Below: *Competing in a steeplechase race at Ludlow in October 1980*

Prince Charles is very conscious of some people's opposition to fox-hunting, and he is seldom photographed riding to hounds. For him the thrill comes simply through galloping and jumping in rough country, in the company of good friends

African safari

Above: *An historic meeting—Prince Charles and Princess Anne with the late President Jomo Kenyatta of Kenya. On the right is Ngina Kenyatta, the President's wife. Charles and Anne were invited to coffee at the Kenyattas' home in Gatundu, near Nairobi, during their two-week holiday in Africa*
Below: *On the last day of his visit, Prince Charles visited the mobile clinic of the Flying Doctor service in Nairobi. Here he is meeting a mother and her baby from the Masai tribe*

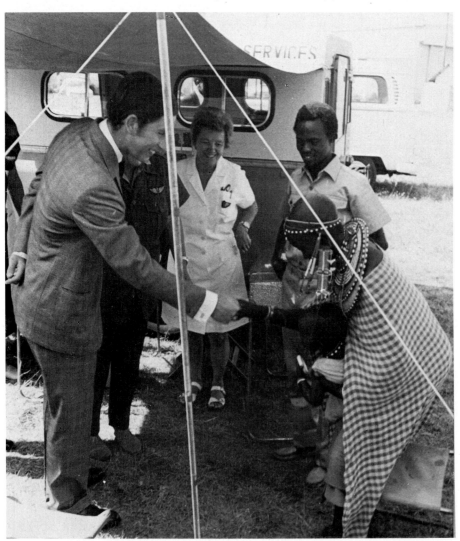

"My idea of a holiday," said Prince Charles, "is to do all the things you do if you are not on holiday. I like going off and being energetic, running round in circles and generally appearing absolutely mad."

He was speaking to newsmen at the end of a four-day camel trek in Kenya's northern frontier district during which he had walked more than 50 miles, slept under the stars, and been startled by an uninvited rhinoceros blundering around only 40 feet from his sleeping bag.

This was in February 1971, when he and Princess Anne had joined forces for a two-week private and first visit to Africa.

While Anne was busy making a documentary film for the BBC's Blue Peter programme, in aid of the Save The Children Fund, Charles went off on his safari, accompanied by his Private Secretary and one or two local experts. First stop was a fishing lodge on Lake Rudolf, but then it was on and out to the dry plains of the northern frontier.

"The fun of it is one could really walk about the bush and come across animals suddenly, and watch them.

"The people who looked after our camels, and the game scouts, thought I was absolutely mad being in a dried-up piece of country instead of sitting in a hotel and letting the animals come to me. But I like going off somewhere really wild and seeing it before it has lodges built all over it."

When he returned, unshaven, two ostrich feathers stuck in his bush hat, he looked to be in his element. Resting in the shade of a clump of thorn trees the Prince reflected: "That was something I really enjoyed. It was the best thing I've ever done, or one of the best, the sort of enlightened masochism which I go in for."

But even though this was a private visit to Kenya there were official, though pleasant, duties to be done. Prince Charles visited a hospital and had tea with the nurses. Princess Anne visited a Scottish church and talked with boy scouts. Together they took coffee with the late President Kenyatta at Gatundu. And in Nairobi, Prince Charles, with the special authority of the Queen, bestowed the first knighthood of his life, dubbing the President of the East African Court of Appeal.

When they arrived back at London's Heathrow Airport on a rain-swept February night Charles and his sister went straight on to Windsor for a family reunion. In their luggage were lots of photographs of their travels. But, with Charles at least, no cinefilm. "I don't take cine because one can bore the backsides off people."

*"I like going off somewhere really wild and seeing it before it has lodges built all over it,"
said Prince Charles after a four-day camel trek in the north of Kenya.
It was his and Princess Anne's first visit to Africa. Together they travelled through a game
reserve, and while Charles was on his own safari
his sister made a documentary film in aid of the Save The Children Fund*

Big brother to Andrew and Edward

The Queen always wanted more than two children. But because she came to the Throne at a much earlier age than she had expected—she was only 25 when her father died, in 1952—she put off having more children after Charles and Anne, until she had settled into her new role.

Prince Andrew was born in February 1960, and Prince Edward four years later—when the Queen was almost 38—making him 16 years younger than Prince Charles.

The age gap between Charles and his brothers meant, as it would in any family, that for the first few years he was very much the "big brother", and they were toddlers in the nursery. He was, after all, a senior boy at Gordonstoun when his youngest brother was born.

But from the time Andrew and then Edward started school themselves Charles has taken the role of eldest brother very responsibly. When he was away for months at a time with the Royal Navy his letters home always asked for news of Andrew and Edward, and he looked forward to receiving the newest batch of photos taken by his mother. He also wrote frequently to the boys, chiding or congratulating them on school exam results.

In character, it is said that Andrew is a mixture of his father and his sister while Edward, an altogether gentler boy, reminds people of his grandfather, King George VI. In the last year or two Prince Andrew has developed into an exceedingly handsome and dashing young man, who looks as if he might still be "a bit of a handful"—the description of him given by the mother of a French family with whom he stayed for a few weeks as a young teenager.

He appears to have none of the shyness that his elder brother had to overcome, nor did he seemingly display to his schoolfriends in Scotland and Canada an overabundance of modesty.

He is a forceful personality, made attractive to many by an accompanying sense of humour which often takes the form of practical jokes. He expressed no desire to follow his elder brother into university—always preferring that he should one day be a pilot in the RAF or Navy. His relations with his elder brother probably owe a lot to his admiration of Prince Charles as a pilot, ship's captain, and fearless polo-player.

Prince Andrew is second-in-line to the Throne which means that, until Prince Charles has a son of his own, Andrew's position will be increasingly important. And what many people often forget is that both King George VI and King George V—Andrew's grandfather and great-grandfather—were also born second-in-line, but each eventually came to the Throne.

Left: *Charles, Anne and Andrew, arriving at Clarence House in August 1960 to wish their grandmother, the Queen Mother, a happy 60th birthday*

Right: *Six-year-old Prince Andrew and his elder brother setting off from Liverpool Street station for Christmas at Sandringham*

Below left: *Andrew and Edward returning from Sandringham in January 1973, in charge of the royal corgis*

Below: *Prince Charles and his brothers engrossed in a game of pinball at Sandringham*

Far left: *The 11-year-old Prince Charles holds, very carefully, the infant Prince Andrew in his arms*

Below left: *The whole family gathered together at Frogmore, Windsor, in 1965. The grounds of Frogmore were designed in 1793, but in subsequent years the garden became overgrown, until it was redesigned after World War I under the guidance of the late Queen Mary*

Above left: *Prince Edward tries out his hand at driving at Windsor, guided by big brother*

Left: *Christmas holidays at Sandringham, and Prince Edward comes to hear Charles practising the cello, which he first started playing at Gordonstoun*

Above: *At Buckingham Palace on Remembrance Day, 1976*

Below: *The three brothers, leaving the Braemar Games during the family summer holiday at Balmoral in 1973*

Right, above: *On board Britannia during a visit to Canada in July 1976*

Right: *Charles joins Andrew on a parachute course at Brize Norton in 1978*

Talking to...speaking at

The Queen has never given an interview to an author or journalist, and it is unlikely that she ever will. Prince Charles, on the other hand, has done several radio, television and press interviews over a space of years. He has also made two speeches in the House of Lords, and taken a major role in almost a dozen television documentaries. Making use of the media in a variety of ways ties in with his views on modern monarchy, that it should never be thought to be too remote. *Or too familiar.* He turns down far more invitations than he accepts—on average, up till now, he has given only one major interview every 18 months—and it says something for the willing candour of the Prince (to say nothing of the skill of the interviewers) that we know as much about his personal views as we do.

For instance, we have discovered, over the years, that Charles is enthusiastic about outdoor sports, but would not be too keen to try rock-climbing. Women's liberationists annoy him because they tend to argue all the time. He enjoys reading, but has a tendency to drop off to sleep over a book; he likes classical rather than pop music; believes strongly in conservation but gets pleasure out of hunting and shooting. He would not like to see the Queen abdicate. He would like to have a home in Scotland after he's married. And the only time he has refused point-blank to answer a question was when he was asked whether or not he wore pyjamas in bed! "My great problem," he told one interviewer, "is that if I do express views I'm then held to those views for the rest of my life virtually."

In common with every other member of the Royal Family he is careful not to say anything that is politically controversial. This restriction on his liberty, which does not appear to affect the tenor of Prince Philip's speeches, is something that Charles evidently accepts. And he has overcome the natural fear of speaking in public which, he admits, terrified him at first. "The only time I still get slightly nervous is when I sense the audience is slightly hostile" (this really happened only once—when he made his first visit to Wales as a student), "or if I turn up at an occasion and have to make a speech when there doesn't seem to be anything you can say."

The Prince has always insisted on writing his own speeches. He is painstaking in his research and, like all good public speakers, uses humour to win over his audience. Addressing 5,000 members of the Institute of Directors when he was only 22 he confessed that the idea of speaking for 30 minutes had alarmed him. "How on earth am I going to keep all those overworked and underpaid people awake all that time? Whoever invited me exploited my extreme naivety and innocence."

After his maiden speech to the House of Lords, Lord Shepherd, Leader of the Lords, declared: "In all my experience in this House I do not recall a speech of such character, so beautifully delivered."

The last time that an heir to the Throne had delivered a speech from the floor of the Lords was in 1884 when the Prince of Wales—later Edward VII—spoke during a debate on housing for the poor.

Prince Charles chose a less controversial topic—sport and leisure—but in recent years he has tended to be more outspoken.

In 1979 he told Australian scientists in Canberra that the Russian writer, Alexander Solzhenitsyn, was right to see a lack of courage in the West. "I doubt he is exaggerating when he talks about a decline in courage being possibly the most striking feature which an outside observer notices in the West nowadays." In the same year, arguing for an end to industrial conflict, he told a trade union conference: "When we try, we can knock the stuffing out of all our competitors."

Like others in the Royal Family, Prince Charles has a cautious attitude towards a Press that reports almost his every word and action. He told the Guild of British Newspaper Editors in Cambridge, in 1980: "My particular concern is that freedom becomes, all too easily, licence . . . The world is in a sensitive situation, and so much depends on the way news and comment is reported."

The Scottish
Prince of Wales

"I adore Scotland almost more than anywhere else," Prince Charles once told an interviewer. And he would like to have his own house in the Highlands, where he and his wife could live for at least a month or two each year, and where eventually they could share family holidays with their children— just like those Prince Charles himself has enjoyed at Balmoral since he was a baby.

Prince Albert bought Balmoral for Queen Victoria, and both of them were idyllically happy with the frequently cold, misty weather and the draughts that seem capable of penetrating even the thickest walls.

Edward VII found it altogether too cold a place and his son, George V, preferred Sandringham: "the place I love better than anywhere in the world". But the Queen and Prince Philip have passed some of their happiest days in Scotland. They spent part of their honeymoon in the Queen Mother's Deeside home—and their eldest son shares their almost passionate regard for the rugged countryside and the bracing air.

Actually, apart from his annual holidays at Balmoral, Prince Charles has spent quite a surprising amount of time in Scotland. There were his five years at Gordonstoun, and a good proportion of his time as commander of HMS Bronington was spent at Rosyth, near Edinburgh.

While he was there he spent much of his shore-leave visiting friends in the area, or going to parties. Indeed every mother with a young unmarried daughter was always anxious to have Prince Charles accept an invitation to dinner or a dance. A few of them were lucky!

Like the Queen—who does, after all, boast a Scottish mother—Prince Charles not only feels at home among Scots but holds very strong views on Scotland's place within the United Kingdom. Facing questions at a Royal Commonwealth Society meeting in London in June 1977 he was asked about the changes he expected "when you become King of England."

". . . Britain!", interrupted an unsmiling Prince.

Far left: *A delightfully informal shot of Prince Charles with his cousin, Lady Sarah Armstrong-Jones, at Balmoral*

Above: *The tartan rugs, the studded walking shoes of Prince Philip, the corgi, and the Queen holding a toy for baby Prince Andrew. The picture was taken at Balmoral in 1960*

Right: *Visiting a dairy farm on Balmoral estate in 1957*

Below left: *Coming ashore from the royal yacht for a holiday in Scotland*

Below: *The traditional royal visit to the Braemar Highland Games, which take place each summer. On this occasion Prince Charles was nearly seven years old*

Coronation

A coronation is a fairly rare event in the world today, simply because there are few countries where kings or queens still reign.

Nepal has a king—Birendra Bir Bikram Shah Dev, Incarnation of Vishnu, King of Kings, the Five Times Godly, Valorous Warrior and Divine Emperor. He was crowned in February, 1975, in his mountain capital of Katmandu, and Prince Charles attended the ceremony, representing the Queen. Also invited were the Duke and Duchess of Gloucester and Lord Louis Mountbatten, former Viceroy of India.

To western eyes a Nepalese coronation is not only dazzling in colour, but also a trifle bizarre in its traditions.

Part of the ceremony at King Birendra's coronation involved ritual daubing of the King with mud collected from the top of a

Top left: *At exactly 8.37 a.m.—the moment deemed auspicious by court astrologers—the chief priest crowns the King*
Middle left: *King Birendra and Queen Aishwarya on the throne of writhing golden cobras*
Left: *Lord Louis Mountbatten, former Viceroy of India, and Prince Charles wearing honours bestowed by King Birendra*
Above: *Crown Prince Deependra, three-year-old heir to Nepal's throne*
Above right: *The pagoda-roofed Hanuman Dhoka palace, once the residence of the Shah kings who, in the 18th century, established control over what is now Nepal*
Right: *The crowning ceremony lasted some four hours in all*
Far right: *The ceremony over, the King and Queen are carried in procession through Katmandu in a scarlet and gold howdah atop a gaudily painted elephant*

in Nepal

mountain, the bottom of a lake, the tusk of an elephant, the floor of a cowshed and the doorstep of a harlot's house.

The King was cleansed with butter, milk, yogurt, and honey, then priests chanted to him: "You are the uterus of government, you are the womb of government, you are the vagina of government, you are the navel of government".

The Prince of Wales was given a place of honour in front of the actual coronation pavilion to which the King formally progressed after the ritual anointing. The Prince wore naval uniform and a Nepalese decoration conferred on him by King Birendra shortly before the coronation.

King Birendra is the world's only Hindu monarch and the 10th successor to the Shah dynasty which founded modern Nepal. He actually ascended the throne on the death of his father in 1972. Among his guests at the coronation three years later were four masters and 15 former pupils of Eton—the King's old school. They, along with everyone else, had to rise early on coronation day, for the crowning could only take place at a moment deemed auspicious—and the court astrologers placed this moment at 8.37 a.m. precisely.

The crowning ceremony took place in a thatched pavilion where King Birendra and his Queen, Aishwarya, sat on a throne of writhing golden cobras which rested on the skins of lions, tigers, leopards, deer and oxen, symbolising the monarch's sovereignty over the animal kingdom.

Sonorous chanting of ancient hymns mingled with the droning of conches and the shrill piping of wood-winds, while servants used yak-tail whisks to freshen the air.

The whole ceremony took so long—about four hours—that officials kept footmen bobbing around, serving tea and biscuits to the heavily bemedalled and perspiring onlookers. Afterwards the King and Queen rode through Katmandu on a gaudily painted elephant, applauded by many thousands of the King's 12 million subjects.

The jamboree is said to have cost a total of £4 million—an extravagant slice of the annual budget of this small and underdeveloped country.

As part of the national celebrations the Nepalese government announced pardons for some 400 criminals. The pardon extended to murderers, rapists and cow-killers. In a further act of benevolence the King announced that he had instructed his government to make primary education free for every Nepalese boy and girl. Quite separately, the King's guests from Eton College decided on another novel present— they clubbed together to endow a scholarship at Nepal's only university for a student from a poor part of the country.

The Comedian

Humour being very much a question of personal preference, it is thought by many that Prince Charles can be very amusing, while others are sometimes left wondering what all the laughter is about. Some people have a similar reaction to the Goons (Charles listened to those radio buffoons avidly at Gordonstoun, and their wacky unreality still appeals to him).

When you are a prince it may be comparatively easy to make people laugh—the press, particularly, seize on any impromptu aside as if it were pure Oscar Wilde—but it is not so easy to be genuinely funny or original.

Prince Charles' strong points are mimicry and thinking up practical jokes. As a pupil at Cheam he was allegedly responsible for going into the cloakroom and switching around his fellow-pupils' caps on the pegs, so that when the boys came to leave, everyone got the wrong cap and confusion resulted . . .

During his service in the RAF the Prince arranged for a loudspeaker announcement calling on cadets to hand in their shoes because a fault had been detected in the heels. Several fell for the prank before realising the date was April 1 . . .

And on another occasion Charles arrived at a Master Tailors' dinner wearing an old hacking jacket over his stiff white waistcoat and Order of the Garter decorations. This was his way of responding to the trade paper that had recently criticised the Prince for his "cult of shabbiness". After the saying of grace—and amid roars of appreciation from the diners—Charles removed the jacket to reveal a perfectly tailored evening suit. If ever Prince Charles were in a position to need publicity he would easily know the best way to go about obtaining it.

Most people first became aware of Charles' gift for amateur acting when he appeared, two years running, in a Cambridge University revue.

Dressing up and delivering two-line jokes was something he enjoyed immensely. It was a natural progression from the charades he played with the Royal Family over Christmas—though the double entendre of some of the jokes might have been frowned on in some quarters.

As a cello-playing pop star, just out of gaol for smoking chicory, he was described as "the biggest plucker in the business". As the Duke of Wellington, hearing that the French had retreated from the plain of Waterloo: "Thank God. They've made a hell of a mess of the playing fields." But the biggest laugh of all came when Charles, dressed as a Victorian reprobate, flung his arm round the waist of a pretty gipsy and marched off stage with the exit-line: "I like giving myself heirs."

Since Cambridge Prince Charles has had little or no chance of being the "ham actor"—except in a piece of historical documentary film (which was mainly about flying) where he played his favourite role of Goon. But he is still always ready with the wisecrack aside, or the in-joke in a speech, and his timing is excellent. All of which is very welcome, for the thought of an heir to the Throne without any sense of humour is almost too terrible to contemplate.

Far left: *In a Cambridge university revue Prince Charles gets a custard pie in the face*

Above: *After watching Roy Castle perform on a wobbly "fun" bike during the opening show at the Churchill Theatre, Bromley, Kent, Prince Charles asked if he could have a go*

Above right: *Taking a lesson in tap dancing from comedians Morecambe and Wise during a charity performance which raised £10,000 in aid of the Queen's Jubilee Appeal*

Left and right: *Rehearsing a typical piece of Chaplinesque goonery with a set of bagpipes for a Trinity College revue. The title of the revue, staged when Charles was up at Cambridge in 1970, was Quiet Flows The Don, and the particular sketch was called "Going for a quick one"*

Representing the Queen

Many, many times in the coming years it will fall to Prince Charles to represent the Queen as Head of State on ceremonial occasions. Sometimes the occasion will be sad, as when he attends the funeral of a world leader. At other times the event will be a celebration, tinged with regret for only a few. One such event took place in July 1973 when, as a serving officer aboard the frigate HMS Minerva, he took leave to land at Nassau and officiate at the independence celebrations of the Bahamas. Even at 24 years old he was a practised hand—this would be his third "handing back" ceremony.

At midnight the Union Jack was lowered after 244 years of British rule of the Bahamas, and Prince Charles was present to see the birth of another piece of the world that could look after itself. The Bahamas, with its population of 168,000, was the 33rd member of the Commonwealth to receive independence since World War II.

The ceremony was unique in at least one respect. For just as the Prime Minister, Lynden Pindling, was in the middle of his speech a cable parted with a loud "ping", and the gold and blue striped canopy descended on the platform party. The wife of Sir John Paul, interim Governor General, came off worst, but fortunately was only stunned. Prince Charles, two seats away,

made sure she was all right, then joined in the laughter of the 15,000 spectators massed in Nassau's main sports stadium.

The independence celebrations lasted for five days, and Prince Charles stayed to the end. On his arrival he had told a huge welcoming crowd that his ship had visited several parts of the Bahamas and he had fallen "hopelessly in love" with the islands.

"It provided me with an opportunity to discover the peace and fascination of life on a Bahamian beach—something which I had never experienced before and which gave me great happiness and contentment."

On the night before his departure the Prince did a round of three separate state balls at exotic beach hotels, partnering several ladies in energetic dancing. In one dance, with the attractive wife of the Prime Minister, he gyrated with twisting hips and flailing arms—and the other guests stood back to admire. It was another occasion on which the Prince had shown he had lost all trace of shyness of his youth.

Much more recently, in April 1980, Prince Charles represented the Queen at a politically sensitive programme of independence celebrations—this time in Salisbury in Africa, where the Union Jack was lowered for the last time, to be replaced by the flag of Zimbabwe. As ever, Prince Charles behaved

Above: *Taking the salute at the Bahamas independence celebrations in July 1973*

Below: *Prince Charles delivers the Queen's message to the people of the Bahamas on arriving in Nassau. On the left is the last British Governor, Sir John Paul*

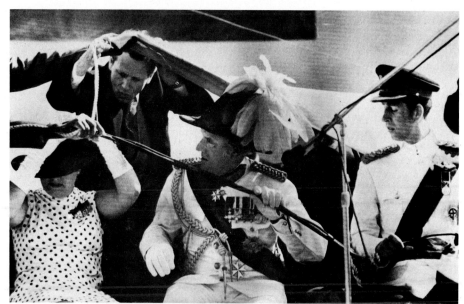

Above: *Stepping ashore on arrival in the Bahamas from HMS Minerva*
Below: *The independence celebration cake*
Bottom: *Dancing with Mrs. Marguerite Pindling, wife of the Prime Minister*
Right: *The collapse of the canopy!*
Below right: *Inspecting the guard of honour*

REPRESENTING THE QUEEN *continued*

impeccably in a situation tense with the undercurrent of feeling following a bitter eight-year war between black and white, and a period of 14 years when Britain's last African colony, under Ian Smith, had defied Whitehall rule.

In Salisbury a crowd of 35,000 shouted their approval as, on the stroke of midnight, the flag representing the 89 years of white rule was lowered and the multicoloured standard of the new state of Zimbabwe was raised.

In a message to the white community, the new Prime Minister, Robert Mugabe, urged adaptation to the political change, and a feeling of brothers bound to one another by a bond of national comradeship. "If yesterday I fought you as an enemy," he said, "today you have become a friend. If yesterday you hated me, today you cannot avoid the love that binds you to me and me to you."

Police used tear gas to control enthusiastic crowds of Africans trying to get into the football stadium where the independence ceremony took place. But otherwise the celebrations were unmarred by violence and the jubilation over independence was apparent everywhere.

In his speech marking the formal transfer of power, Prince Charles expressed hopes for the future in these words: "To heal what has been hurt and wounded, to reunite what has been divided, and to reconcile where there has been enmity is the finest foundation on which to rebuild and increase the quality of life in your unique country."

Right: *Standing beside Lord Soames, Prince Charles salutes the end of an era as the Union Jack is lowered for the last time at Government House in Salisbury*
Below left: *Inspecting a guard of honour at Salisbury airport before returning home*
Below right: *Prince Charles receives an Independence Medal from Robert Mugabe, Zimbabwe's first Prime Minister*

The Duke of Cornwall

The eldest son of the monarch is, by charter of 1337, automatically Duke of Cornwall, whereas he is Prince of Wales only by royal decree. And if the sovereign has only daughters, then the revenue from the Duchy lands and properties goes to the Crown.

Edward III created his son the first Duke of Cornwall in the 14th century, when the boy was six. The estates that fell to him and his successors were at first mainly in Cornwall, but ownership extended over the centuries and the Duchy now comprises almost 135,000 acres, spreading from the Scilly Isles in the west, Gloucester to the north, and Wiltshire and Dorset to the east. There are even 45 Duchy-owned acres in London—in Kennington, south of Lambeth Palace, where the Black Prince once hunted and Test cricketers now play at the Oval. The bulk of the estates of 68,000 acres is on Dartmoor, and includes the prison which pays ground rent to the Duchy.

When Prince Charles toured the Duchy shortly after his 25th birthday much play was made of the feudal dues that, on ancient paper at least, are still in force. At Launceston, Cornwall, a forester presented him with a load of firewood as rent, and the mayor brought a pound of pepper.

In the manor of Fordington, Dorset, there is a tradition for villagers to roast a sheep on the village green every St. George's Day, and supposedly send a leg of lamb to the Prince.

But though he is fond of tradition, Prince Charles is also keen that the farms, woodlands, mines and quarries in the Duchy should be run as efficiently, and happily, as possible. He pays careful attention to the regular reports he receives from the staff at the administrative headquarters of the Duchy at Buckingham Gate, in London. In 1975 over £400,000 was spent on repairs and general upkeep of Duchy property and land, and the income from the Home Farm more than doubled, thanks largely to expansion and the introduction of modern methods of agriculture.

When he visits the Scilly Isles, usually arriving by helicopter and without any publicity, he stays in a three-bedroomed bungalow, called Tamarisk, hidden from public view by high walls, but only a few yards from the impressive granite building housing the Duchy's provincial offices.

Up till now Prince Charles has derived the majority of his wealth from the income of the Duchy of Cornwall. In 1978 this income amounted to over £2,000,000. But outgoings totalled very nearly as much. Prince Charles' share was £256,382, half of which he paid over to the Treasury in accordance with an arrangement he made when he became 21—an arrangement, incidentally, which was subject to review if he married.

Above: *Arriving in the Duchy of Cornwall, and waving to some of his tenants*

Below: *Heading for the Duchy offices in London, to preside over a meeting of the Prince's council*

Right: *Chatting to Kennington flat-dwellers in the London borough that forms part of the Duchy estates*

Above: *Headquarters of the Duchy of Cornwall on the Isles of Scilly*

Below: *The view from the offices*

Left: *Chatting to the children of tenants*

Bottom: *On a walk-around in his Duchy*

Above: *About to put his signature to yet another document, this time in the town hall on St. Mary's, one of the Scilly Isles*

Right: *He appears alone, but apart from the photographer there must be, as always, his detective nearby*

Below: *Aboard the Scilly Isles lifeboat*

LONG LIVE PRINCE CHARLE[S]

To Ghana and the Ivory Coast

Prince Charles, to no-one's surprise, is an ardent believer in the idea of the Commonwealth. "If you believe in what it can do, you can make it do great things."

And when he makes an official visit to a Commonwealth country he is very conscious of the fact that his visit is planned not only to help foster relations between that country and Britain, but also to encourage international trade.

In March 1977 Prince Charles spent 11 days in Ghana and the Ivory Coast, and at the conclusion was enthusiastic about the warmth and friendliness of everyone. He described his feelings thus: "I felt at home the moment I stepped off the plane in Ghana. That is one of the great things about visiting Commonwealth countries."

The main event on his crowded schedule was the 50th anniversary celebration of Achimota School, sometimes called "the Eton of West Africa". Co-educational, with 1,500 pupils, it was designed to combine the best English standards of English education with the emphasis based on African tribal traditions.

The two aspects of the school were symbolised at the Jubilee durbar at which the Prince sat on a dais flanked by local tribal chiefs. He inspected a guard of honour from the typically British-style army cadet force, then watched displays of African dancing by different tribal groups.

In contrast, a couple of days later Prince Charles was photographed wearing a striped mini-kaftan, with fly whisk and ceremonial cane when he was made an honorary chief of a tribe on the fringe of the Sahara desert in the far north of Ghana.

In almost overpowering heat and humidity, the Prince spent the final three days of his trip in the Ivory Coast—the first major royal visit to French-speaking Africa. To his surprise and delight Charles was greeted by thousands of people dancing and singing in the streets.

Britain is a big buyer of Ivory Coast bananas, pineapples, cocoa and coffee, but at the time did not match its imports with exports. Following the Prince's visit it was hoped that trade would improve.

Opposite—**Top left:** *Amidst a sea of black faces at Achimota School, Ghana*
Top right: *The umbrellas are to stave off the sun, as tribal chiefs wait to greet the Prince*
Left: *On the estate of the President of the Ivory Coast, where Prince Charles was a private guest*
Above left: *A double arrowhead of motor cyclists escorts the royal car through the streets of Abidjan in the Ivory Coast*
Oval: *A toast to the Queen at the state banquet in Accra*
Below: *In the Ivory Coast Prince Charles is shown round a pineapple farm by the wife of the manager*

A PRINCE'S STYLE *continued*

"bunches" (the trade name for swatches of different kinds of cloth) to the Prince at the Palace for his approval. He has his own ideas as well as current fashion, cut and material. He likes stripes, flannels, a 3½ in. lapel, and is keen on single-breasted jackets. In 1981 he was wearing the fashionable parallel trouser legs and he rarely has turn-ups now. The royal taste, says his tailor, is subdued and traditional, definitely not flashy.

The Prince's shirt-makers, Turnbull & Asser Ltd. in Jermyn Street, London, is possibly London's most elegant men's shop. Mr. Cuss of the Bespoke Department describes the Prince favouring Windsor collars like those of his father and grandfather, with cufflinks or buttons on the cuffs.

Off duty, Prince Charles dresses like his contemporaries; in wide baggy cord trousers and wellington boots for country walks, many-pocketed anoraks for fishing expeditions, and tweeds for weekends.

He appears to have a large drawer full of T-shirts. When he left HMS Bronington at the end of his naval career, he gave a T-shirt to each member of the crew, apparently designed by himself, with the insignia of HMS Bronington on the chest, and "Smile" on the back.

He has been voted on to both the best and worst-dressed international lists. But unlike his younger brother Andrew, who can get away with really trendy clothes in public, Charles must dress to suit the part.

Occasionally he will put on "fancy dress" as a good-mannered gesture to a host country, as happened when he turned up at a rodeo in Canada, in cowboy gear and a 10-gallon hat.

Although it looked spontaneous, the Prince's measurements had been sent ahead of the royal tour party so that the hat didn't fall over his eyes, and the cowboy boots didn't pinch.

It's important that a dressed man, royal no less than any other, must not only look good but feel good.

Above: *Resplendent in striped mini-kaftan, with fly whisk and ceremonial cane, Prince Charles was made an honorary chief of a tribe on the fringe of the Sahara Desert in northern Ghana*
Below left: *Lady Charlotte Manners, daughter of the Duke of Rutland, wears Cuban-heel suede boots, while her partner sports monogrammed casuals*
Below: *A former student himself, he is now installed as Chancellor of the University of Wales. The ceremony took place in July 1977*

Above: *Photographed in the Grand Hall, Windsor Castle, in the uniform of a Colonel of the Welsh Guards, tunic order*

Left: *A Colonel in the Welsh Guards, frock coat*

Below left: *In service dress, Colonel-in-Chief, Royal Regiment of Wales. Prince Charles also wears his military wings, medal ribbons of the Order of the Bath and the Coronation Medal, and the Star of the Order of the Garter*

Below, centre: *Naval wings on his sleeve, Prince Charles in the uniform of a Commander in the Royal Navy*

Below: *Wearing the uniform of a Wing Commander in the Royal Air Force. The decoration round his neck is the Knight Grand Cross of the Bath*

127

George III – a favourite ancestor

More than once, Prince Charles has spoken of his high regard for King George III whose reign of almost 60 years, from 1760, was the longest of any king in Britain's history.

"I think to a certain extent," Prince Charles told writer Douglas Keay in 1975, "one is a combination of all one's ancestors in either a larger or smaller part, and I do slightly associate myself with King George III because I happen to admire and appreciate and sympathise with a lot of the things he did and enjoyed."

According to Chambers's Encyclopaedia, George III was mentally retarded in childhood, neurotic in youth, and in manhood became liable to attacks of insanity. And in the view of one historian at least, "he inflicted more profound and enduring injuries upon his country than any other modern English king".

But Prince Charles thinks, basically, his ancestor has had a raw deal from historians, and he is always glad to come to the defence of the King.

"He was a great patron of the arts, of music and science. And above all he was a great human being. He had a sense of humour, and one of the main things about him was that he was loved very much, certainly towards the end of his reign, by the vast majority of his subjects. He had this wonderful ability to get on with people. He was basically an English country gentleman. He was called Farmer George, which was a great compliment in many ways."

George III died in 1820 at the age of 81, having meandered through the last 10 years of his life totally mad, and blind as well. But, in common with recent scholarly opinion, Prince Charles does not believe that the King was a manic-depressive or a schizophrenic.

"I think it's been fairly conclusively proved," he told Alistair Cooke in a televised conversation in 1976, "that he suffered from a metabolic condition (porphyria) which affected the blood and which then affected, to a certain extent, his mind. He had hallucinations more than manic attacks."

Prince Charles agrees that he does partly think of the King as a model for himself "because I believe very strongly that one can learn a great deal from history. The whole of life is based on what happened before. It enables us to interpret the present and the future." During George III's lifetime, the world underwent two major upheavals—the end of Britain's rule over the American colonies, and the French Revolution. And Prince Charles has already lived through at least one event, the formation of the European Community, which future historians may see as just as important.

Antonia Fraser, in an introduction to John Clarke's biography of George III, wrote: "As the reign proceeded, George III's strongly-held religious faith, combined with his own evident probity provided a much-needed stabilising influence in an age of European chaos; while his private interests, whether botany, prison reform or Sunday schools, were all in some way aimed at enhancing the quality of English life."

It is, perhaps, not so difficult to see why Prince Charles admires his great-great-great great-great grandfather.

Above: *A portrait of King George III, from the studio of Allan Ramsay—painted around 1767 it now hangs in the National Portrait Gallery, London*

Right: *Published in 1816 by Thomas Kelly, this engraving shows the King in a stance and costume reminiscent of Napoleon, who was defeated the previous year at the Battle of Waterloo*

Right: *An engraving published in the European Magazine in 1820. It was drawn by Wivell from a model in wax by Burch*

Below: *King George III at the age of 73, eight years before his death. The aquatint is by J. Sadler*

Sailing at Cowes, Isle of Wight— traditional home of yachtsmen—in 1972
Oval: Trying archery at the Landowners' Game Fair at Abergavenny in August 1976

The sporting Prince

Unlike Prince Andrew, his young brother, Prince Charles was not born with a natural flair for athletic sport. As a small boy he was quite tubby, and any aggression—he was not a bad boxer—resulted from frustration and a determination to stand up for himself.

Prince Philip taught his son to swim, in the pool at Buckingham Palace, and gave Charles his first lessons in sailing on Loch Muick, near Balmoral. Other, more controversial sports were introduced as part of the traditional upbringing for any son of a landed gentleman. Prince Charles shot his first woodcock, on the Sandringham estate, when he was 12. And before his 14th birthday, he had stalked and killed his first stag on the hills above Balmoral.

The Prince seems to be attracted to sports that are either solitary and tranquil, or extremely physical and generally noisy. Although he has played several times for Young England in international polo matches, Prince Charles is not inclined towards "team games". He prefers to pit his skills and nerve against the elements, or the wiliness of creatures in the wild.

He gets a thrill from surf-riding, but derives just as much pleasure from the slow and individual business of trout and salmon fishing—he is reckoned now to be the most skilled rod in the Royal Family, excelling even the Queen Mother.

Each August he slips away to Iceland for two weeks of fishing—two weeks which he looks forward to increasingly each year. And sometimes, with his grandmother, he pleasantly passes other days casting for salmon on the River Dee in Aberdeenshire.

He doesn't like golf or tennis very much. Football, which he played at Cheam, doesn't excite him. He prefers to play rather than to spectate, and if the sport doesn't arouse any interest in him—well, there are plenty of other things for him to get on with.

Apart possibly from polo, which he takes very seriously, Prince Charles tends to think of his sports as hobbies. But his other interests include playing the cello, and painting in water colours. He brushes aside his talent as an artist—"jolly useful for Christmas presents"—and tends to think of himself as badly out of practice when it comes to cello-playing. As a young man he learned a bit about playing the trumpet—again, a brash contrast to the breathtaking sound of the cello—but more recently there has seemed to be less and less time for uninterrupted relaxation.

Above left: *The 16-year-old Prince went on a ski-ing holiday with his father and sister in Liechtenstein*
Above: *Trying his luck with clay pigeons, at the Royal Bath Show in June 1977*
Left: *As a child Prince Charles was much more nervous of horses than was his young sister*
Below: *During a visit to Athens for King Constantine's wedding, Prince Charles showed his prowess as a diver by upsetting a raft carrying unauthorised photographers. But at least one cameraman managed to get his picture first*

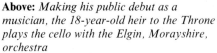

Above: *Making his public debut as a musician, the 18-year-old heir to the Throne plays the cello with the Elgin, Morayshire, orchestra*

Left: *Taking part in a British Driving Society competition at Smith's Lawn, Windsor, in June 1976*

Below left: *At the Abergavenny Landowners' Game Fair in August 1976 Prince Charles attempted sports, known and unfamiliar to him*

Below: *An unusual sight: Prince Charles in trilby, here photographing the Queen*

Above: *Wearing borrowed size 10 boots, Prince Charles played a light-hearted game of cricket against the world's top Grand Prix drivers in 1968*

Left: *At the same cricket match, Prince Charles knocked up 20 runs before being caught by Bruce McLaren off Graham Hill, who is seen here playing at slip*

Below: *The Prince, at the tiller of the famous Cowslip*

The Prince of Wales marries . . . 1863

Left: The bridegroom wore the uniform of a general under a cloak of the Order of the Garter. The bride's gown was trimmed with Honiton lace

Above: The wedding cake, made in Chester

Below: The wedding took place in St. George's Chapel, Windsor. Queen Victoria watched from an alcove, hidden from general view

What Queen Victoria had required for her son was a wife of "good looks, health, education, character, intellect and good disposition." Her eldest daughter Victoria, Crown Princess of Prussia, helped in the search and came up with Princess Anna of Hesse, "very favourable"; Princess Marie of Hohenzollern-Sigmaringen, "quite lovely"—but a Roman-Catholic; Princess Marie of Altenburg, "shockingly dressed"; and Princess Alexandrine of Prussia, "not clever or pretty". The Prince of Wales didn't care for any of them.

But then his parents were recommended to the 17-year-old Princess Alexandra of Schleswig-Holstein-Sonderburg-Glucksburg, daughter of Prince Christian of Denmark. Queen Victoria was sent a photograph and declared that Alexandra was, indeed, *unverschämt hübsch*—"outrageously beautiful". Prince Albert warned his son that "it would be a thousand pities if you were to lose her." And so, without much enthusiasm, "Bertie" went to see the girl at a contrived meeting.

He found her pleasant, pretty in face and figure, but still felt he wasn't ready for marriage. "I don't think he is capable of enthusiasm about anything in the world," wrote his disappointed mother. The Prince Consort, driven almost to despair by his son's reluctance to marry, subsequently became ill and died of typhoid fever.

The following September, 1862—a couple of months before the Prince of Wales' 21st birthday—his engagement with Princess Alexandra was finally announced. And by now he plainly was in love. "I indeed now know what it is to be really happy," he told his doctor, "though I dare say I have never done anything to deserve it."

Queen Victoria tended to agree. However, she was extremely pleased with Alexandra. But as the day of the wedding—March 10, 1863—approached, she became more and more desolate over the loss of her own husband. She decided she could not take part in the procession to St. George's Chapel in Windsor Castle, but would witness the ceremony, dressed in mourning, from a wooden alcove near the altar that had been built by Henry VIII.

Princess Alexandra made a beautiful bride—in contrast to her bridesmaids who, according to Lady Geraldine Somerset, were "eight as ugly girls as you could wish to see." The bridegroom, 5 ft. 7 in. but looking taller because of built-up heels, wore the uniform of a general under the cloak of the Order of the Garter.

The Royal Family and their guests took luncheon in the Castle afterwards—though the Queen still preferred to eat alone in another room.

Later, she stood at a window in the Grand Corridor and waited for the bridal couple to leave. When the Prince of Wales saw her, he halted the carriage and he and the Princess stood and bowed to the Queen. They then continued on their way to a week's honeymoon, on the Isle of Wight. And, on their return, Queen Victoria wrote: "Alix looked so sweet and lovely at luncheon, and Bertie so brightened up."

Canadian journey...

Prince Charles' visit to the rugged landscape of central Canada in July 1977 provided press photographers with a field-day.

The Prince had gone to Alberta to take part in centenary celebrations commemorating a treaty signed in Queen Victoria's name, whereby local Indians handed over some 50,000 square miles to the white man, in return for everlasting support of one kind or another.

In front of Prince Charles the present-day Blackfoot tribe, led by Chief Jim Shot Both Sides, made it plain in speeches that they didn't think all that much of what they'd got out of the "everlasting support".

But then, seemingly letting bygones be bygones—for the duration of the visit at least—they invited Prince Charles to smoke a pipe of peace. He gladly obliged—even though he had some difficulty extracting any smoke from it. A few minutes later Big Rain Cloud opened and he and the official party were drenched to the skin.

The next day, on the Blood Indian reserves at Stand Off, Southern Alberta—where 95 per cent of the Blood Indians are on welfare—Prince Charles was conducted on the usual tour of show-places, introduced to local VIPs and asked to unveil a statue of the legendary Chief of the Bloods, Red Crow.

Then after a light lunch, where it took some time for anyone to notice that the guest of honour hadn't got a plate, the Prince was installed as an honorary Kainai chieftain—following in the footsteps of his great-uncle, the late Duke of Windsor, who was the first white man to be so honoured.

For the photographers especially, this was the high point of the trip. Close-ups of the Prince having his face painted in red and yellow stripes by the Chief Medicine Man . . . Putting on the huge head-dress of eagle feathers . . . Being presented with a peace pipe, a hand-made saddle and a horse called Cross Bell . . . these are the kind of pictures that keep press photographers clicking-happy. Prince Charles is used to dressing up to please, and even joined in a little rhythmic Indian dancing to round the whole thing off.

After meeting the Indians, the next item on the itinerary was to meet the Cowboys and attend the world-famous Calgary Stampede. For this he was joined by his brother Prince Andrew, each of them wearing enormous white stetsons and string ties round their necks. Prince Charles, sitting high in his Western saddle on a big, black horse, rode ahead of the Stampede parade past a screaming, swooning crowd of hundreds and thousands.

Prince Andrew at one point was penned-in by a clutch of Canadian beauties, and did nothing but flash them all a dazzling smile.

Altogether, it was probably one of the most successful trips Prince Charles has made. For the young and old alike, the chance to see the two brothers together—reminiscent, some said, of Butch Cassidy and the Sundance Kid—was, as one reveller commented: "Real dandy".

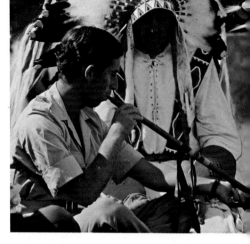

Above: *A non-smoker, Prince Charles obligingly smokes a pipe of peace*
Below: *The brothers—Prince Andrew joined Prince Charles at the Calgary Stampede and they both wore the almost obligatory stetsons*
Opposite—Top left: *Unveiling the statue of the legendary Chief of the Bloods*

Left: *Looking at the penned steers and broncos*
Below: *Sharing a joke with modern Indian chiefs and their wives, who were dressed in traditional costume for this occasion*
Opposite—Top right: *Dressed as an honorary Kainai chieftain*
Bottom left: *100 years ago Queen Victoria signed a treaty with these men's ancestors*
Bottom right: *A royal ride-about*

American dream...

Left: *At San Antonio, Texas, a peaceful glide down the river on a colourful barge* Below (left to right): *Before a gala dinner in Hollywood, posing with Farrah Fawcett-Majors, left, Sophia Loren and Cary Grant. A hurriedly arranged "round-up" (for the benefit of the press) at the Texas ranch of Tobin Armstrong and his wife Anne, formerly U.S. ambassador to Britain—a busy main road was only 15 yards away. At St. Louis, Prince Charles paused to have a word with the bespectacled commander of present-day citizens dressed up in the army style of American independence year— 1776. Straight from the set, two of the stars of M.A.S.H., the long-running television series, enjoy the informality of a pre-lunch drinks party in Hollywood where they were introduced to Prince Charles*

Prince Charles' jet-hopping tour through America in October 1977 was probably the most exhausting trip he has made so far. It was also one of the most successful.

In 12 days he visited 11 cities, starting off in Chicago, ending up in San Francisco. Often he put in a 16-hour day. At the end he joked to reporters: "I've shaken hands with so many people I need a hand transplant."

The "glad-handing" began in Chicago where hundreds of thousands of well-wishers, most of them women, packed the pavements trying to catch even a glimpse of the Prince as he walked for nearly a mile down one of the main streets. "Only General McArthur and Elvis Presley ever had a reception like this," said one veteran cop.

At a civic reception, recalling the late and famous Mayor Daley of Chicago, Prince Charles recalled: "When my mother last visited Chicago in 1959 the Mayor said she should come back and bring the kids. She's not here, but I guess I'm here as a kind of elderly kid."

The Queen's "elderly kid" flew on to Cleveland, Ohio next, and the customary round of tree-planting, visits to a steel mill and a university. As in Chicago, and later on in San Francisco, he ran into small groups of IRA supporters. At Cleveland State University, as he was about to address a sombre set of lawyers, a third-year student stood up and demanded to know "when England was going to stop torturing political prisoners."

The questioner was quietly escorted from the hall, and the ensuing tension was broken by Charles asking: "Before I begin, are there any other Irish here?"

All along the way Americans warmed to Charles' easy manner. Whenever he made an ad-lib comment, sometimes at the expense of a local dignatory, nearly everyone—including the dignatory—talked about "His Royal Highness's dry English wit." They particularly liked the way he very modestly began almost every speech by saying he was an expert on nothing.

In Atlanta, Georgia, southern belles—or, more likely, their mothers on behalf of the daughters—had for weeks made strenuous efforts to be invited to the Governor's Mansion for a five-course dinner with the Prince. But in the end Charles sat at a table with the Governor and his wife, and other politicians and their wives. Among the few young people present, apart from the guest of honour, were Chip and Jack Carter, sons of the American President.

Following a lightning trip to Charleston and a visit to an American football game in Athens, Prince Charles was due to spend a leisurely Sunday at the Texas ranch of Anne Armstrong, former U.S. ambassador to Britain, and her husband. But a mini "cattle-round-up" was laid-on for the press before Charles had a chance of indulging in a hard-fought game of polo. In the evening the Armstrongs entertained their guest to a magnificent barbecue under the stars.

At the Houston space centre the next day Charles inspected capsules, sat in a replica of the "buggy" that went to the moon, and tried his skill "flying" two approaches in a space-shuttle simulator. Early the following morning, when he watched the shuttle Enterprise do the real thing he was wryly amused that the pilot also made a slightly bumpy landing, as he had done.

Probably the most enjoyable day of the whole tour was spent in San Antonio, Texas, where Charles went aboard a flower be-decked barge for a slow river ride. This followed a visit to the historic Alamo.

One of the main purposes behind any royal tour is to promote friendly relations and increase trade between Britain and the host country. In Los Angeles, addressing the World Affairs Council, Prince Charles produced figures to prove that Britain's industrial record was not as bad as is often made out. "In an average year, 98 per cent of the factories in the United Kingdom could expect to be strike-free," he said.

In contrast to the visits to industrial plants and space centres, the Prince paid a call on Hollywood, took lunch with Lauren Bacall (and many other stars), and at a gala dinner the same evening sat between television's Farrah Fawcett-Majors, an ex-Charlie's Angel, and Angie Dickinson, of Police Woman.

After the tour had ended up with three days in San Francisco, one American bystander observed: "Prince Charles could come over here any time he liked and we'd vote him into office straightaway. The people really love him."

...and a new world

Thanks to marauding photographers, whenever Prince Charles has been to a hot, sunny clime, the pictures that have been printed back home are usually those of him being kissed by a girl, chased along a beach in his swimming shorts, or shimmying to the swaying rhythm of a South American samba. Presumably things would be different once he got married . . .

But, in any case, the pictures gave a slightly false impression.

On a visit to Brazil in March 1978, for instance, Prince Charles was invited to a dinner at the town hall in Rio de Janeiro where entertainment was provided for the 1,000 guests by the Beija Flor Samba School, top prize winners at the Rio Carnival.

Invited to join in, the Prince hesitantly took to the floor with a dancer wearing the flimsiest of glittering silver costumes. The television and press cameramen could hardly believe their luck!

Predictably, the pictures appeared all over the world. But, almost as predictably, there

was hardly a mention anywhere of the Prince's tour of the Brazilian Navy and a visit to an English school the same day, or the fact that the next day he was to tour industrial complexes in São Paulo.

To the outsider, and especially from a distance, overseas Royal tours look like a lot of fun. But behind the glamour there is usually serious intent—the Foreign Office would hardly be likely to foot the bill otherwise! Generally, the underlying objective is to improve international relations, or to give trade a boost.

While Prince Charles was in Brazil, a London newspaper claimed that he had accepted an offer from a consortium of British businessmen to become a £50,000 a year roving salesman. The story was angrily denied.

But by happy chance, only a few days later, a group of British banks completed a deal to invest in a huge steel mill near Rio, with an expected return of £11 million. And nobody denied that Prince Charles' presence

in the country had helped "clinch" the deal. On the same tour, after he had visited a Venezuelan gold mine, a British firm landed the contract to modify the gold ore treatment plant. "I am sure the Prince's visit speeded things up," said a well-satisfied chief executive of the company later.

And in Brasilia, the Prince promised an influential audience that when he returned home, "I will do my best to persuade British businessmen that this country has a splendid and exciting future economically, and that it is well worthwhile getting involved."

Visits to Commonwealth countries, like Prince Charles' to Australia in 1979, are less to do with "showing the flag" and much more to do with "sharing the flag".

Usually they are tied in with commemorative celebrations. In 1979 the Prince crossed to the other side of the world to join in Western Australia's celebration of 150 years as a European settlement.

Western Australia covers an area three times the size of Texas, stretching to almost

one million square miles. Prince Charles travelled the length and breadth, covering over 5,000 miles in 16 days and visiting 20 towns. Such was his attraction that in the small town of Derby practically the entire population drove the dusty 10 miles out of town to greet the Prince at the tiny local airport.

Australians don't content themselves with just ogling royalty. Whenever possible they like to chat to them—a much more informal approach than that of the British.

Even so, some thought the informality went a little too far when a lithesome Perth model, Jane Priest, made sure of getting publicity when she took the Prince by surprise and planted a smacker of a kiss as he emerged from a swim in the ocean.

Later, following a parliamentary lunch in Canberra, Prince Charles spoke warmly of his school days in Australia during the Sixties which, he said, had left him with a lasting appreciation of life Down Under.

And, he added with a smile: "I also like to think that it laid the foundation for that feeling which enables some ladies to dispense with the formalities usually associated with greeting royalty.

"I would raise no objection were this particular form of greeting to become a formality . . ."

Left: *Prince Charles stopped the show when he joined an exotically-clad Brazilian dancer for an energetic samba session. The occasion was a dinner at Rio de Janeiro's town hall during Charles' tour of 1978*

Above: *Essential wear for the Australian bush during Prince Charles' tour of Western Australia in 1979—a swagman's hat, complete with bobbing corks on strings.*

Right: *From the same tour—Perth model Jane Priest caught up with Charles and gave him a smacking kiss. The picture appeared in newspapers around the world*

Among the souvenirs

PRINCE OF WALES

With the exception, strangely enough, of the birth of a royal baby, practically every other milestone in royal history—such as a coronation or a wedding—is used as an excuse by manufacturers to flood the market with a load of romantic keepsakes. Some are, by any standards, trashy—and others are in just as bad taste but much more expensive. But whatever the articles themselves are like, the people who buy them are happy—so where's the harm?—and they will hand down the souvenirs, chipped or cracked, from generation to generation, to adorn mantelpiece or wall.

The wedding of Prince Charles will undoubtedly produce its own avalanche of bric-a-brac, and it will be interesting to spot which, if any, of the souvenirs will become sought-after antiques in a few years' time.

When he signed the visitors' book on his first trip to America, the Prince of Wales, later Edward VIII, could never have guessed that the picture taken of him would subsequently be used to adorn thousands of keepsakes, from cigarette boxes to buttons. And what about the souvenir designer who put an extra ring on Prince Philip's naval uniform—making him a commander, a rank he never held? Anyone with a jug or a plate with that particular picture on it may find the souvenir is worth a lot more than was originally paid for it.

Top: *A World War I keepsake of the Prince of Wales,
later Edward VIII, printed on silk and measuring only three inches by four*
Above: *A collection of cartes de visites from Edward VII's
early days, and postcards from a later
generation, including one showing Edward VIII and the Queen as a young girl*

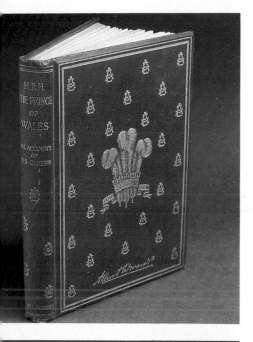

Above: *Plaster cameos of Prince Albert, later Edward VII, and his bride, Princess Alexandra*
Right: *A jug celebrating their silver wedding*
Below: *A collection of souvenirs including a button-brooch sold to raise money for sailors, and a rosette commemorating the wedding of the Prince of Wales and Princess Alexandra*

Top: *"HRH The Prince of Wales, An account of his career"*
Above: *The picture used on the cigarette box was taken during a visit to America in the days of Prohibition. The Prince was signing a visitors' book when someone asked: "Are you taking the pledge?"*
Below: *A biscuit tin showing the Prince of Wales, later Edward VIII, with views of the Empire on the sides*

Above: *The Prince of Wales feathers on a Victorian jelly mould*
Right: *The programme for "a cinema performance" at Government House, Calcutta.*
Below: *Not a shaving mug, but a lemon squeezer*

Below: *A glass tankard commemorating the Prince of Wales' investiture in 1969*
Right: *One of the hundreds of approved designs to commemorate Prince Charles' investiture at Caernarvon castle*

Adventure unlimited

One of the more enviable benefits of his position, Prince Charles recognises, is the opportunity to attempt a wide variety of exploits that are denied to almost everyone else. Who else can say that, before reaching 30, he had piloted a jet, commanded a ship, parachuted into the sea, swum underneath the Arctic ice, been on an African safari, and gone round the world? Who, for that matter, would have the courage and tenacity to achieve so many goals?

Prince Charles enjoys meeting a challenge, not head-on but with careful preparation and sensible regard for safety.

"I try to be as responsible as I can about the things I do because I'm totally aware there are people who will have to take the can if something goes wrong. On the other hand, I do feel strongly that in my position I must set an example. I must show people that I am prepared to do things that they are expected to do. Perhaps it's because I'm constantly feeling that I have to justify myself, my existence. I want to prove to myself that I can accept challenges, and that I can mentally accept things which are perhaps dangerous or slightly frightening."

Certainly the most spectacular of his exploits took place in 1975 when he flew to Frobisher Bay to visit the North-West Territories of Canada. He started by sweeping across the snow in a husky-drawn sled in search of caribou. This was at Grise Fiord, the most northerly Eskimo settlement within the Arctic Circle. Then, at the underwater-research station at Resolute Bay, he descended through a hole in the frozen Arctic that began to freeze over again as he went down. His guide was Dr. Joe MacInnis, a research scientist who is credited with being the first man to swim beneath the North Pole. The ice was six feet thick, the water temperature 28.5 degrees Fahrenheit, and the sea-bed 30 feet below. Without protective clothing a man who went into that water would be dead within a few minutes.

Prince Charles wore a "variable volume" diving suit, and was so fascinated by the world beneath the ice that he stayed down for half an hour. When he finally surfaced he was almost euphoric. He delighted photographers (and gave the Queen Mother great amusement when she saw the pictures) by inflating his diving suit to enormous proportions before letting it down slowly so that he seemed to shrink like a deflated balloon.

"Swimming under the Arctic was fascinating," he said later. "I wouldn't have missed that opportunity for anything."

To the critics who say that as heir to the Throne he shouldn't subject himself to

Above: *The 26-year-old Prince of Wales undergoing a commando endurance course at the Royal Marines depot at Lympstone, in Devon*

Left: *After scaling climbing nets and vertical walls, edging along catwalks and swinging across chasms, Prince Charles crawled along this rope and,* **below,** *waded through freezing waters. Afterwards he described the whole experience as "a most horrifying expedition"*

unnecessary risks, Prince Charles responds: "I've spent my life being instructed by one person or another, in every sort of field. And I've learned that if you do exactly what the man says nothing will go wrong. And it's your own fault nine times out of ten if it does."

Stringent precautions are taken, obviously, whenever Prince Charles participates in any operation that carries an in-built risk. Rehearsals and tests are carried out beforehand. The aeroplanes and helicopters he uses, belonging to the Queen's Flight, are scrupulously maintained. But no previous heir to the Throne has made as much use of flying as has Charles, who prefers to pilot himself rather than be passenger. The Queen and her eldest son never travel in the same aircraft. And though precautions are taken, the risks run by Royalty today are necessarily greater than they were in the past.

As far as new experiences are concerned, Charles has already achieved many of his ambitions. Some—such as hang-gliding and piloting a jet, as opposed to a helicopter, on to an aircraft carrier—will probably always be denied him because of the risk factor. Other new ventures, with no risk involved, centre around travel. Prince Charles loves seeing new places and faces—one visit he'd especially like to make is to the Galapagos Islands. In the years ahead he is bound to have the opportunity for travel, adventure, and ever-widening experience of human behaviour.

Above left: *Over Poole harbour, Dorset, Prince Charles makes his first parachute jump*
Left: *In a Force Five wind, in South Wales in 1970, the Prince takes part in a sea-rescue exercise*
Top: *The moment before he dives under the Arctic ice in April 1975*
Above: *Preparing for the dive, in specially heated suits*
Below: *A royal walkabout, in ice and snow*
Right: *On the same visit, at an oil rig*

Silver Jubilee

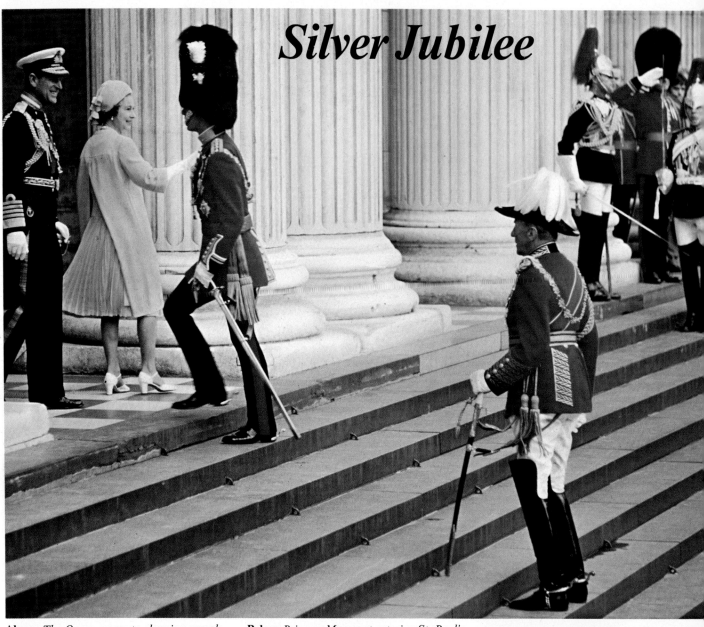

Above: *The Queen waves to cheering crowds before entering St. Paul's Cathedral for a service of thanksgiving*
Below: *The Queen Mother with her grandsons*

Below: *Princess Margaret entering St. Paul's*
Right: *Prince Charles, Princess Anne and Captain Mark Phillips, listening to the Archbishop of Canterbury's address*

Above: *According to tradition, the Royal Family comes out on to the balcony of Buckingham Palace after the Jubilee thanksgiving service at St. Paul's Cathedral*

Right: *At St. Paul's, everyone kneels—but Prince Charles is prevented, by his tight uniform and spurs*

Below: *"We want the Queen," was the thunderous cry of the thousands crowding against the gates of Buckingham Palace on Silver Jubilee Day*

The Silver Jubilee of the Queen's reign, in 1977, was an event that filled Prince Charles with an enormous sense of pride. Besides being very close to his mother as a person, he also greatly admires the way she performs her role as monarch. He is one of the very few people who is in a position to see the Queen immediately *after* the procession is over or the tour to the shipyard completed.

He is often there to catch her expression in that moment when she turns and goes inside, after waving from the balcony of Buckingham Palace to thousands of well-wishers, at the end of a seven or eight-hour day of constant scrutiny.

He knows about the strain, appreciates the dedication, admires the sheer strength and the overwhelming sense of purpose that the Queen possesses.

What must have delighted him more than anything was the realisation that the Silver Jubilee celebrations showed that the mass of the people, subjects of the Queen like himself, felt the same way as he did.

The celebrations—almost a year of pageantry, royal walkabouts and thousands of street parties up and down the country—were highlighted on June 7 when the Queen went in procession to St. Paul's Cathedral for a Silver Jubilee service of thanksgiving.

Crowds lined the route eight deep to watch the Gold State Coach—built in 1762 and last used at the Queen's coronation—as it trundled majestically through the streets of London.

An estimated figure of 500 million television viewers saw the Queen and Prince Philip proceed down the centre aisle of the Cathedral and take their places at the head of a congregation gathered together from all parts of the world. Then they heard the ▶

Archbishop of Canterbury, Dr. Donald Coggan, put into words what all of them felt:

"Our nation and Commonwealth have been blessed beyond measure by having at their heart an example of service untiringly done, of duty faithfully fulfilled, and of a home life stable and wonderfully happy. For this we thank God. From this we take courage."

There were loved and familiar hymns, and prayers that really meant something—Prince Charles and Captain Mark Phillips couldn't kneel because of their tight uniforms and long spurs—but the most exciting and human touches of the whole day came when the Queen walked from the Cathedral to Guildhall for lunch. All along the route small children sprang out from the crowds offering crayon pictures and posies of flowers to their Queen.

"We came because we love you," people told her. Visibly moved by the spontaneous surge of affection, the Queen smiled, and looked 10 years younger. Perhaps, like her grandfather at his Silver Jubilee celebrations, she had not fully realised how the people really felt about her.

A few days later, when the euphoria had subsided and everyone was comparing memories, Prince Charles confessed that he had twice nearly fallen off his horse during the procession from Buckingham Palace to St. Paul's, when he rode behind the Gold State Coach.

"I forgot we were due to stop at Temple Bar, and was mesmerised by the wheels of the coach and trying to keep the right distance. Suddenly the coach stopped and I nearly fell off."

The second tricky moment came when he arrived at St. Paul's, expecting a mounting block to help him dismount. Unfortunately the block was put under the horse instead of at the side. "I missed it and nearly fell to the ground."

There must have been a score of near-mishaps in a day of ceremony and celebrations which had been planned down to the last detail. But at the end of the day, when thousands of well-wishers surged to the railings of Buckingham Palace, the lasting impression was one of sweeping love and enthusiasm for the Royal Family, among young and old alike.

The organiser of a "Stuff the Jubilee" rally told a reporter: "We were going to have a proper meeting with food and drink, and then march on Buckingham Palace to proclaim the republic. But, unfortunately, it was too cold and only five people managed to turn up . . ."

Left: *Being entertained at Deptford on the Queen's tour from Greenwich to Lambeth*
Above: *One way of getting a vantage point to watch the celebrations is to straddle a pram!*

Centre: *A typical Jubilee street party—one of many that were held all over the country*
Oval: *The Trooping the Colour ceremony took its traditional place in the Royal calendar*
Far right: *The biggest firework display since the Coronation was held after the river procession*

Uncle Dickie

"He had that quality of real moral courage, of being able to tackle unpleasant tasks. That is, in these days, a rare quality indeed. He had it in abundance. It is one of the reasons I adored him."

In these words Prince Charles described Lord Louis Mountbatten in his address to a congregation of 2,000 at the memorial service to his great-uncle at St. Paul's Cathedral in December 1979.

Lord Mountbatten—Uncle Dickie to the family—had been Prince Charles' hero and friend since he was a small child. After the death of his grandfather, King George VI, when Charles was still a toddler, Lord Louis practically took his place.

It was he who urged the Prince's parents, at the invitation of the Prime Minister, Harold Wilson, on a Cambridge university education after he left Gordonstoun, followed by entry to the Royal Navy.

"Trinity College, like his grandfather; Dartmouth like his father and grandfather; and then to sea in the Royal Navy, ending up with a command of his own." The advice, like the man who gave it, was adventuresome and decisive.

Prince Charles loves his father, but at times in his life he has been slightly in awe of him. His great-uncle was the person he could always turn to for advice, for heart-to-heart talks, and for weekends away from the claustrophobia of the Palace down at Broadlands, the Mountbatten family home, in Hampshire, where he was always made very welcome.

Mountbatten's daughter and son-in-law, Lord and Lady Brabourne, welcomed him, too, at their holiday home on the Caribbean island of Eleuthera. Their son, Norton Knatchbull, had been at Gordonstoun with Charles, and their two daughters were also good friends. Indeed, it had long been a secret hope of Mountbatten, it was suspected, that one of these girls might one day become the Princess of Wales—after all, in the 1940s, Mountbatten's nephew, a Lieutenant in the Royal Navy, had successfully wooed the future Queen Elizabeth . . .

But this was not the reason great-uncle and grand-nephew were such good friends. Mountbatten admired Charles' sense of duty and honour, and Charles was inspired, amused and perhaps in later years, only occasionally exasperated by Mountbatten's really extraordinary self-confidence and boundless enthusiasm.

When, on August 27, 1979, the news came through from Ireland that this brilliant commander-in-chief and last Viceroy of India had been blown up by the IRA while puttering about in a holiday boat with his family . . . not only Prince Charles, but practically the whole world was outraged.

"He was a family man," Prince Charles observed at the memorial service. "He was a devoted husband, an enlightened father, a wonderful grandfather, and a very special great-uncle . . . There could be no finer tribute to a man than that so many people loved him."

The elder statesman of the Royal Family, Earl Mountbatten of Burma—Uncle Dickie—was always a close and much-loved friend to his great-nephew Charles

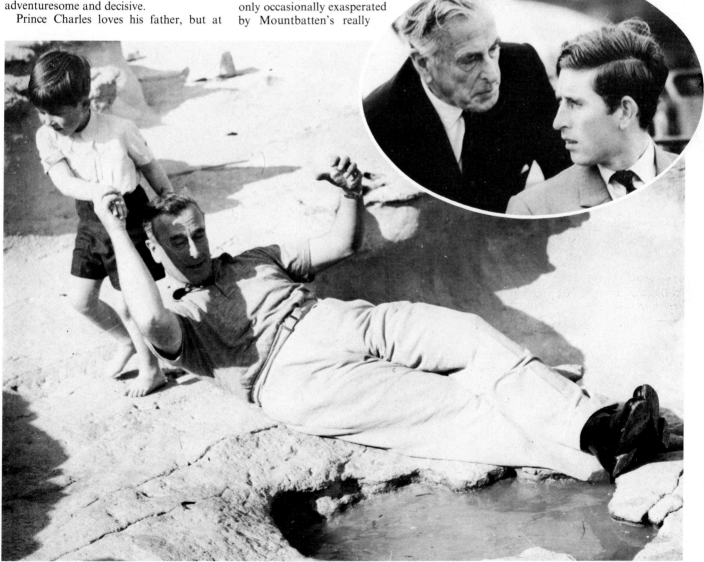

The way they were

The highlight of any wedding ritual is the bridal gown. And when the bride is royal, "the dress" takes on a particular significance. The embroidery might conceal emblems of constitutional relevance, the fabric—is it woven from silk spun by British silk worms? Emanuel, the designers of Lady Diana's dress, are now established for life after receiving the royal commission.

Before the detailed media coverage given to royal events today, the dresses of princesses and queens were seen by the general public only in the sketches in ladies' magazines. A pity, since some of them were masterpieces. The young Queen Victoria wore white satin, with a flounce of Honiton lace—not by any standards elaborate, more an extreme crinoline. The orange blossoms on her head matched the trimmings on her train, which was tended by bridesmaids in billowing dresses with extremely revealing necklines.

Prince Charles' great-grandmother, Queen Mary, was married in a heatwave, and judging by the pictures of her diminutive, corseted waistline, the young Princess May must have been made of strong stuff! Her dress was of embroidered silver and white brocade, her jewels all diamonds.

The Queen Mother's wedding dress followed the looser lines of the day in fine chiffon moiré. The longer train—worn under one lent by Queen Mary—was of Nottingham lace, chosen to boost ailing home sales of lace.

Our present Queen's dress was designed by the late Norman Hartnell. It reflected the more extravagant New Look of a world released from wartime clothing restrictions. In ivory duchesse satin, the skirt was almost circular and embroidered in pearls, crystals and beads.

Princess Margaret, married at 29, broke a good many royal fashion conventions. Her dress, although designed by master embroiderer Norman Hartnell, was of simple white silk organza—not a bead in sight. It reflected the growing awareness of the television camera and the bride presented a stunning silhouette from every angle.

Princess Anne's was perhaps the first truly "media" wedding. The photographs could have come straight from the set of a television play, or from the posed fashion pages of a glossy magazine. Maureen Baker, of the wholesale fashion house of Susan Small, was the thoroughly modern designer chosen by the thoroughly modern princess. The dress was high-necked, almost prim, with bodice tucks emphasising her beautifully slim figure.

Above: *In the Chapel Royal, St. James's Palace, the young Queen Victoria wore the collar of the Garter around her waist, heavy diamond and sapphire jewellery at her neck*
Right: *Queen Mary, as the young Princess May of Teck, caused a stir with her mother's veil—a wisp of lace that covered neither shoulders nor face*

Top left: *The centre panel of the Queen Mother's 1920s dress was heavily embroidered with pearls and beads. By contrast, Princess Margaret (left) chose the stark simplicity of silk organza.*
Top right: *The Queen's immense court train echoes the motifs on her dress*
Above: *Princess Anne's dress was a simple classic with the minimum of detail*

*Thirty years together . . . the Queen and her devoted
son at the Braemar Highland Gathering, 1978*

The first official public appearance of the Prince of Wales and Lady Diana Spencer, at the Goldsmiths' Hall, London, on March 9. They were attending a function in aid of the Royal Opera House Development Appeal Fund

The start of a new life . . . Prince Charles and his bride-to-be on their engagement day, February 24, 1981

157

"Marriage is a much more important business than just falling in love . . . Essentially you must be good friends and love, I'm sure, will grow out of that friendship and become deeper and deeper."

Prince Charles, in an interview with Douglas Keay for Woman's Own, October 1975

"Next to Prince Charles, I can't go wrong. He's there with me."

Lady Diana Spencer, in an interview for BBC Television News, February 1981

Photographic Contributors